THE VALLEY OF FLOWERS

The Ultimate Guide to an Adventure Trek in the Upper Himalaya

SUSAN JAGANNATH

Dandinik Media

You can download additional material to share the experience of the trek from:

http://www.susanjagannath.com/vof-bonus

If you would like to contact me, you can email me at
susan@susanjagannath.com

Jagannath, Susan. The Valley of Flowers: The Ultimate Guide to an Adventure Trek in the Upper Himalaya. Susan Jagannath. Kindle Edition. All rights reserved.

ISBN 9780648854302

CONTENTS

FOREWORD

In 1931, a party of British mountaineers staggered out of a blinding snowstorm into a sheltered Himalayan valley, blanketed by thousands of flowers and surrounded by a ring of soaring peaks.

This was the Bhyundar Valley, henceforth known as the Valley of Flowers. Frank Smythe's book, "The Valley of Flowers, An Adventure in the Upper Himalaya", an exquisite ode to this secret corner of the mountains was the only book about this hidden gem.

Hidden no more though, as you can get there by helicopter in a single day. But you still must walk the last 5 kms. Unlike the pre – 2013 routes where you meandered up a sloping valley to reach the vale, a steep ascent awaits the trekker today.

In the monsoon of 2019, a party of four friends set out in the footsteps of Frank Smythe to explore the Valley. This book is the result of that foray to access the high Himalayas, where the valley nestles high among the glacier-encrusted, cloud kissed peaks.

FOREWORD

This is the second edition of this book, updated for safe hiking in a world where the COVID-19 virus is still active.

PART I

Essential Details for your Adventure

CHAPTER 1
MOUNTAIN BLOOMS
CLEAR-RUNNING STREAMS

> *Often, in dark winter days, I wandered in spirit to these flowerful pastures with their clear-running streams set against a frieze of silver birches and shining snow peaks.*
>
> — *Frank Smythe*

High in the mountains, among windswept peaks and gleaming glaciers is a hidden bower that touches the sky. Like a fragrant benediction among the sacred peaks of the Himalayas, it remained hidden until the last century. Despite the ancient pilgrim paths nearby, this valley stayed the exclusive preserve of flower-munching mountain goats and silent shepherds on their way through the valleys and passes to the dry hills of Tibet.

The rocky path to the high-altitude glacial valley is steep, slippery and soggy. To see the flowers, you must trek through the rains of the monsoon into the swirling cloud-covered reaches of the upper Himalayas. Even then entrance is restricted to a few short daylight hours. Dusk is but a brief interlude before darkness falls like a curtain when the sun slips behind the towering walls of the gorge.

A MAGIC LOCATION

The Valley of Flowers National Park is in Garhwal, in Chamoli district, about 595 kilometers from Delhi. The tiny national park, all 87.5 square kilometers of it, is a UNESCO World Heritage Site, as is the nearby Nanda Devi National Park.

The closest airport is about 300 kilometers away, Jolly Grant Airport near Dehradun. The nearest railway stations are Haridwar and Rishikesh, 276 kilometers away. From Rishikesh the only access is by road along the sparkling Ganges, until the confluence at Devprayag where the road clings to the steep sides of the Alaknanda valley.

The northwest to southeast aspect shelters the valley from winds from the frozen north. Open to the wide skies in the summer, the heat from the golden sunlight melts the glaciers that cover the ground for most of the year. But this is India, with its magical life–giving monsoon. 500+ different varieties of alpine flowers explode into bloom from June to August. The flowers germinate, bloom and seed in a 12–week period, in this sky–tossed valley nestled among the spectacular peaks of the Himalayas.

At an altitude that varies between 3000 to 3600 meters, drained by the Pushpavati, the valley is tiny, barely ten kilometers long and two kilometers wide. This does not seem difficult, but at this altitude you are three kilometers vertically up in the sky. It can be hard on lungs, knees and feet, make sure you acclimatize before you go.

CAN I DO THE TREK?

In all instances, check with your doctor before you go. You must climb three steep kilometres at an altitude of 3000m to access the Valley from Ghangaria. You can reach Ghangaria by mule, but using porters to reach the Valley itself is no longer recommended, due to social distancing norms. You can also take a helicopter from Gobind Ghat to Ghangaria, depending on the weather.

After three kilometers on a steep and winding road, the road ends at Pulna village in a melee of organized dung–scented chaos. From Pulna you must trek, or ride a mule to Ghangaria.

From Pulna village it is an 11 – kilometer trek to the base camp at Ghangaria. Given the rigorous ascent, despite a few down slopes, it will take from 4 – 6 hours. Be prepared for rain, slippery surfaces and watch for the ethereal waterfalls, and burgeoning flowers on the way. Also watch out for begging sweepers and mule droppings.

The valley itself, is a steep 3 – 4 kilometers (1.8 miles) from Ghangaria. Although it does not sound too far, plan to stop at Ghangaria and proceed to the valley the next morning.

After the floods of 2013 destroyed the original route, the new path has taken a steeper route. When you arrive gasping at the top of the climb, you must walk for a further 3–5 kilometers at the minimum to experience the full wonder of the Valley of the Flowers.

A SEASONAL FEAST OF FLOWERS

Snow and ice cover the Bhyundar valley or Valley of Flowers from October to May. This includes access to bustling

Ghangaria which turns into a ghost town from October to May.

The season typically starts on June 1st, but the exact date varies.

You can trek from early June until the beginning of October, check exact dates, as it depends on the ice melt. The best time to visit is from mid July to mid August, when the flowers are in full bloom. This is also the wettest part of the year, so add time for road closures.

Day temperatures of 15 to 20 degrees C, falling to 8 to 10 degrees C by night, make for a cool trek. Layer clothing as it can get warm when trekking.

Flowers include the majestic and protected Brahma Kamal, lilies, anemones, primula, and blue poppies. The blooms come in all colors and sizes and change from month to month in subtle waves of color.

Anemone, Geranium, Marsh Marigold, Primula, Potentilla, Aster, Lilium, Himalayan Blue Poppy, Aconite, Delphinium, Ranunculus, Corydalis, Inula, Saussurea, Campanula, Pedicularis, Morina, Impatiens, Bistorta, Ligularia, Anaphalis, Saxifraga, Lobelia, Thermopsis, Trollius, Aquilegia, Codonopsis, Dactylorhiza, Cypripedium, Strawberries and Rhododendrons, Anaphalises and Potentillas, the unfamiliar names hide the sheer beauty of the flowers. These are not the names of dinosaurs, but flowers.

In May when the ice retreats, sweet scented primulas cover the rocky terraces in blue and snow-white anemones light up the valley floor.

With the arrival of monsoons in July, pink and red varieties of flower flush the valley with rosy hues. Balsam, Wallich Geranium, and River Beauty, dominate, although there are plenty of yellow, purple and white flowers.

From late July to the end of August, Pedicularis, Potentilla, Ligularia and many other yellow varieties appear.

More information in Part V.

CHAPTER 2
PREPARING FOR THE TREK
HIGH ALTITUDE

 Today is your day! Your mountain is waiting, So... get on your way!

— *Dr. Seuss*

S teep hikes at high altitudes need significant preparation and information. This chapter describes how to prepare for the trek to the Valley of Flowers, from getting your mindset right and your physical fitness up, to checklists that ensure you leave nothing to chance. The more you prepare, the more fun you will have and the easier the trail. The Valley of Flowers is a series of short walks, but that doesn't mean that it's easy.

You do not need to go with a tour company, but do book accommodation and transportation in advance. See Appendix B for suggestions.

Note: You must check whether the Valley is open, and comply with health requirements put in place. Check with the Uttarakhand State Government portal for up-to-date information. If in doubt, do not travel.

If you have health issues, check with your doctor before you start either the training or the trek.

There are a couple of landlines available from shops in Ghangaria, as Rs 10 per minute. A post paid BSNL mobile may work, however as a tourist, you will not have this.

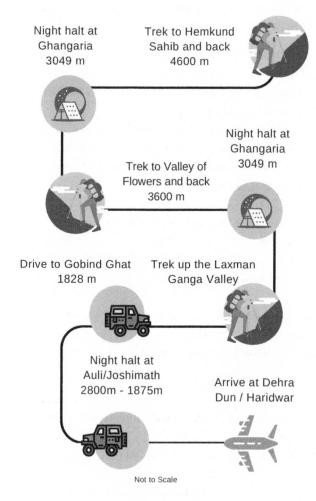

Night halt at
Ghangaria
3049 m

Trek to Hemkund
Sahib and back
4600 m

Night halt at
Ghangaria
3049 m

Trek to Valley of
Flowers and back
3600 m

Drive to Gobind Ghat
1828 m

Trek up the Laxman
Ganga Valley

Night halt at
Auli/Joshimath
2800m - 1875m

Arrive at Dehra
Dun / Haridwar

Not to Scale

The Journey at a Glance

SUGGESTED ITINERARIES

Choose your itinerary first, as it will determine the experience you have, the services you must hire, and your health, before and after the trek.

Five days is needed for this three – kilometer trek, if you want to enjoy it and experience it to the full.

These are the minimal stages:

- Day One – Haridwar or Dehradun to Joshimath – Drive 10 –12 hours
- Day Two – Joshimath to Gobind Ghat to Ghangaria – Drive one hour and trek three to four hours
- Day Three – Ghangaria to the Valley of Flowers – trek six to seven hours.
- Day Four – Ghangaria to Gobind Ghat and Joshimath – Trek three to four hours and drive one hour
- Day Five – Return to Haridwar/Dehra Dun – Drive 10 –12 hours

If you have the time, add an extra day for Valley of Flowers, and another day for Hemkund Sahib. An additional day at Auli will help you to acclimatize.

These are the additional stages:

- Day One – Haridwar or Dehradun to Joshimath – Drive
- Day Two – Joshimath to Gobind Ghat to Ghangaria – Drive and Trek
- Day Three – Ghangaria to the Valley of Flowers – Trek
- Day Four – Ghangaria to the Valley of Flowers – Trek
- Day Five – Ghangaria to Hemkund Sahib – Trek
- Day Six – Ghangaria to Gobind Ghat and Joshimath – Trek and Drive
- Day Seven – Return to Haridwar/Dehradun – Drive

These are the additional stages for a longer trip:

- Day One – Haridwar or Dehradun to Joshimath/Auli
  – Drive
- Day Three –Auli – Trek
- Day Three – Auli/Joshimath to Gobind Ghat to
  Ghangaria – Drive and Trek
- Day Four – Ghangaria to the Valley of Flowers – Trek
- Day Five – Ghangaria to the Valley of Flowers – Trek
- Day Six – Ghangaria to Hemkund Sahib – Trek
- Day Seven – Ghangaria to Gobind Ghat to Joshimath
  via Badrinath and Mana – Trek and Drive
- Day Eight – Return to Haridwar/Dehradun – Drive

These are stages for the desperate or foolhardy:

- Day One – Haridwar or Dehradun to Gobind Ghat –
  Drive 13 – 15 hours
- Day Two – Gobind Ghat to Ghangaria to Hemkund
  to Ghangaria trek eight to ten hours or ride five to
  six hours
- Day Three – Ghangaria to the Valley of Flowers to
  Ghangaria to Gobind Ghat – trek nine to twelve
  hours.
- Day Four – Gobind Ghat to Haridwar– Drive 13 –15
  hours

IT STARTS WITH WHY

When you decide to trek the Valley of Flowers, the first step
is in your mind. Identify why you are doing the trek.

Is it to see the flowers?

Learn about the flowers in the valley, the best time to see them, and your expectations. This is not a man–made exhibition of flowers, this is natural, and you cannot expect all alpine flowers to be big and showy. Many maybe tiny. The flowers differ from week to week. The best time is in the monsoon, so prepare for wet windy weather. Also, for a real botanical experience plan to walk deeper into the Valley, and for this it is better to hire a local guide. You will also need more days, and be ready to climb into the valley on consecutive days. This requires more fitness. If you are taking a porter, then plan for double the cost.

If you are adding Hemkund Sahib, work out the optimal times. Sikh devotees and volunteers throng the path for the opening of the Hemkund *gurudwara* in June. They come in crowds to repair the road and the *gurudwaras,* if you want the hustle and bustle of a true pilgrim experience, this is the time. They will be only too happy if you volunteer to help out.

If prefer a quieter trek, avoid June. This is India, you may find it crowded, or you may be surprised at the emptiness.

If this is for a trekking experience, respect distancing rules. Maintain physical distances when passing others, and wear a mask when you have to be near strangers, for example, when passing each other on the narrow tracks.

GET FIT TO WALK

Because regardless of what you hear or read from other books, walking is not optional if you wish to experience the flowers and higher peaks of the Bhyundar valley. You can get yourself a health coach, or just follow the basic instructions here.

Unless you are already fit and healthy, start your fitness program at least 2 months before you go. If you have any concerns, check with your doctor. Walk 6 days of the week, then take a rest day, and after the rest day, lengthen your walks.

Start by walking a kilometer or less a day.

- By the end of the first week, you should be walking two kilometers a day.
- By the end of the second week, three kilometers in a single stretch.
- In week three, five kilometers a day; and by week four, you should be walking eight kilometers a day.
- In week four, start carrying your backpack. At first, load it up with about two kgs, and every day increase it in small increments, so that by week six you are carrying your full load.
- In week five of your training, walk 10 kilometers on two consecutive days, and on the third day taper back down to five or six kilometers.
- Continue this for the next three weeks of your training, pushing for longer walks every week.
- We did four 15 – kilometer walks in the last two weeks, with full backpacks, and one 20 – kilometer walk.

You might question why you are training hard for a mere three–day walk, the reason is that the trekking stages are steep, so you should be ready to walk at least 12 kilometers a day.

TREK TRAINING FOR THE MONSOON

Train in the clothes, boots, backpacks and water bottles that you intend to use on the trek. Try out the rain gear. Take a lot of rain gear. To see the valley in full bloom you must go in the monsoon, when it rains. All the time. Everyday, and some-times all night.

After your daily walks, the best recovery exercise is the classic yoga waterfall legs up the wall pose. Take off your shoes and socks, sit down on the floor with your right shoulder touching the wall and your legs straight out in front of you parallel to the wall. Pivot your torso so that you are perpendicular to the wall and lie down with your back on the floor. Swivel your hips and legs so that your hips are on the floor touching the wall and your legs are up the wall. You can roll a towel up for support under your hips if needed. Stay there for 10 minutes, then lower your legs sideways to the right, roll onto your right side, and use your left arm to lever yourself off the floor into a seated position before standing up.

What should you do if you can't walk for long periods? Just keep walking as much as you can every day, and solutions will present themselves. But remember that you should talk to your doctor before starting any training, including walking.

Find different terrain to walk in, different from roads and streets. It is all uphill and downhill, find places to walk, and use your weekends well. Explore places where you can find hills and valleys to walk in.

On the days when you can't do the morning walks, start work early so that you can leave early, and walk into the night. However, remember that will and intention are strongest in the morning—if you don't get it done in the morning, you may not get it done in the evening when there are so many excuses!

Wear a hat every day, carry a water bottle and drink a lot of water on your training walks.

TAKE CARE OF YOUR FEET

It is vital that you find the right footwear, and you must break them in before you start the trek. There is a huge range of hiking and walking boots, so keep looking, and trying them on until you find the right pair. It's best to shop for new boots late in the day, after a long walk. Take your socks with you when you try them on.

Look for footwear that will remain comfortable with two layers of socks, one, a thin cotton–polyester blend or bamboo, and two, a wool–synthetic blend. Don't buy pure cotton or pure wool socks as you need socks that wick away moisture from your feet.

I always buy boots which are one size up from my normal size, to accommodate the thick socks, and because feet swell during a long walk. Hiking boots support ankles on tracks that are stony and slippery; boots with enough room at the toes don't hurt your feet on steep downhill treks.

If you already have boots, make sure the tread is good, and check the lacing. Despite all our precautions, one of our party tripped on a hidden rock and the sole peeled neatly away from her boot, and she had no spare boots. After a brief hunt, we found a *mochi* or shoemaker crouched over his awl under a dripping tarpaulin on the streets of Joshimath. If we had been further along it might have not been possible to get it repaired. The young guide in Ghangaria mentioned that she had to go all the way down to Rishikesh to buy good hiking boots.

Wear the boots on your training walks to break them in, and so that you can find and solve problems in advance of your trek. For example, my feet started to hurt too much, and it felt like I was coming up with shin splints or tendonitis. A visit to the podiatrist and a pair of orthotics fixed that in a day or so, and I could continue training.

If you feel blisters coming up, treat them immediately. How do I know if a blister is pending? If you feel any hotspots on your feet, that's the precursor of a blister.

Walking on with blisters is bad for your feet.

NOURISH YOURSELF

Use your trek preparation phase to get fit to walk distances at high altitudes. The best way is to improve nutrition. You will find that the extra exercise curbs your appetite and cravings. If you haven't been taking supplements, consider adding good quality vitamins to your diet.

I took a multivitamin, fish oil and glucosamine every day, and extra vitamin C and Echinacea if anyone in the family was sick with a cold or flu, as we didn't want to fall ill in the run up to the trek. I found that we were more susceptible to flus and colds when we are off the training! The exercise and supplementation make a difference over the long run.

We ate a lot of high–quality protein, with good fats and minimal carbs. This encouraged our systems to burn fat rather than sugar, so we shed some weight in the training, to ensure that we were carrying less weight on our bodies. Extra weight on your hips puts more pressure on your knees and ankles when you are walking every day. One kilogram on your hips is four kilograms on your ankles – that is a lot when you are trekking.

Cut out sugar, limit alcohol and caffeine, and increase your intake of proteins and salad. It's amazing how healthy you eat when you have a clear physical and mental goal.

There is no meat or fish available in the higher reaches of the Himalayas, from Joshimath onwards. Restaurants in Ghangaria may serve eggs, but even these can run out, as everything is carried up on the backs of mules, or porters.

Whatever your current diet, at high altitudes be prepared to switch to lots of carbohydrates and no alcohol. If you have diabetes or other conditions that affect what you can eat, please check with your doctor, and follow instructions.

WATER!

Always carry at least a litre of clean, filtered water with you on your training walk. This is crucial in your training — you must never forget to carry and drink water!

Drink at least 2 – 3 litres of water a day as you train, because you will need it after your walk and throughout the day. As you increase your fitness your body builds more muscle, so you will need more water to flush away any toxins that accumulate after exercise.

Just make sure the you are drinking filtered water, as you don't want to put your kidneys through the extra stress of filtering impure water. Buy or borrow a home water filter before you start your training — this is one of those things that will be with you long after the trek.

Plan to carry a water bottle with you. Don't leave a trail of empty plastic bottles behind you. Please.

CHAPTER 3
PLANNING FOR THE TREK
ANTICIPATION

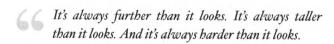
> *It's always further than it looks. It's always taller than it looks. And it's always harder than it looks.*

– Three Rules of Mountaineering

Planning the route of your days in the Himalayas is the important, as it can be difficult to change plans on the go. You can build in other trips along with your Valley of Flowers trek, for example, you can take a day extra to travel up to Gobind Ghat, visiting various river confluences and temples on the way up. After the trek, you can continue to Badrinath and Mana, depending on road conditions.

This chapter also contains information for hiking in the age of the pandemic. The latest information will be in the readers bonus page.

http://www.susanjagannath.com/vof-bonus

INDEPENDENT TRAVELER OR TOUR GROUP

The next decision is whether you are going independently or with a tour group. There are plenty of these about and it is best to go with those who specialize in this area. In which case, your accommodation will be pre–arranged for you.

For the trek, avoid large groups. Do not join group treks with strangers, and if possible avoid public transport after Haridwar or Dehra Dun.

Hire a taxi from a service that assures deep cleaning of the vehicle between passengers, and use the same taxi for the entire journey up and down.

If you opt to go independently, be aware that Ghangaria is a tourist village, so you must pre–book, especially if you are particular about your accommodation.

Free accommodation is available in the pilgrim dormitories of the *gurudwaras* in Gobind Ghat and Ghangaria. The *gurudwaras* also have private rooms at reasonable rates. However, if it is pilgrimage season, it may be difficult to find a place, with scores of Sikh pilgrims walking up to Hemkund Sahib. See Appendix for phone numbers for the *gurudwaras*.

Note: Given the need for physical distancing, it is better to opt for the private rooms rather than communal halls, or crowded hostels.

PLAN YOUR TREK TRANSPORTATION

The next decision is about having your luggage, and maybe yourself transported on the trek sections. Gobind Ghat to Ghangaria, is a moderate to difficult trek, it is not for newbies, or the unprepared.

The following are the stages and my recommendations:

- Gobind Ghat to Pulna – After crossing the bridge, it's a steep 4 kms up the side of the gorge. Take the share taxi.
- Pulna to the bridge at Bhyundar – Moderate, well graded walking path, but with steep twists and turns.
- Hire a *pittoowallah* or porter for your luggage
- Hire a pony for your luggage, or for yourself, and ride up on a well–trained mule accompanied all the way by the *ponywallah* or muleteer.
- Byundar Bridge to Ghangaria Camp – Wind along an uphill path lined with and rhododendron. If the bridge is down, you may have to change ponies/porters here.
- Ghangaria Camp to Ghangaria – A short, but steep climb between towering Himalayan pines, with mossy rocks and flowers peeping out in the undergrowth.
- Ghangaria to Valley of Flowers check point – Upward slope of about half a kilometer. No ponies are allowed.
- Checkpoint to Pushpavati river crossing – Gentle downslopes to boisterous river.
- Pushpavati crossing to Valley of Flowers – steep and winding 1.5 kms, followed by a gentler climb of two kms.

HEALTH & SAFETY

It is safe to walk to the Valley of the Flowers and Hemkund. You can walk alone, or in pairs, or with a group. As usual, take care of your wallet, passport and credit cards by keeping them out of sight and close to you in a travel belt at all times.

Unlike many parts of North India, if you are a woman you will not be harassed or importuned.

There is limited phone coverage after Joshimath. BSNL may work if you have a post-paid account. You can make calls from some shops where they have booths.

If you are using trekking poles, adjust them to your height, and the slope of the land. Longer if you are walking downhill and shorter if you are walking uphill. You can also buy stout wooden walking sticks or staffs from Gobind Ghat, Pulna or Ghangaria. The paths are steep and rocky, so you need to pay attention to every step. Plan your trek days carefully, as you can only trek in the daylight. Tripping and hurting yourself is much more likely in the dark.

Carry snacks and water for the trek. You can buy bottled water in Gobind Ghat, Pulna, Bhyundar village and in Ghangaria.

There are pay toilets along the trekking route to Ghangaria and Hemkund, but there are none in the Valley. You will have to find a bush. Stay away from water ways, as you don't want to pollute the pristine waters.

Ensure that you wear gloves and masks before you enter the toilet, and do not allow your backpack to touch any part of the building. For this reason, it's recommended that you walk with at least one other person, so that you can each look after belongings rather than carry them into the toilets. Carry hand sanitizer, and sanitize your hands after leaving the toilets. Place the mask, if disposable, and gloves into a plastic bag and ensure that you carry your trash with you out of the area.

The *gurudwaras* at Gobind Ghat, Ghangaria and Hemkund provide free treatments for minor ailments. There is also a Government-run basic medical facility at Ghangaria.

HEALTH IN THE AGE OF THE VIRUS

Is there a risk of contracting COVID-19? Yes, there is no point saying that the risk is over. On that note, Uttarakhand had one of the lowest rates of infection, however, the majority of trekkers and pilgrims do tend to come from the virus hotspots, the major cities.

To contain this, entry from particular states may be forbidden, so check before you go. If you are landing in New Delhi, the state is referred to as NCT (National Capital Territory). Mumbai is in the State of Maharashtra, and Kolkata is in the State of West Bengal. The state to the south of Uttarakhand is Uttar Pradesh.

The Indian government, or the State government may require you to install a virus tracking app on your mobile, and may require more certification of your health status.

Follow the protocols of hand-washing, not touching your face, and coughing or sneezing into a tissue or your elbow. Wear a mask in public areas, like when buying food or supplies. Carry your own pen, to use when signing the inevitable documents, use gloves when handling any documents.

Place your phones, identity documents, health documents in clear see through plastic cases, and change them after they have been touched or handled by anyone.

Most importantly, if you have any form of respiratory illness, even a mild cold, do not start the trek. There is very limited medical help in the remote areas, and you may find it difficult to admission to any hospital if you can reach one.

AMS – PREVENTING ACUTE MOUNTAIN SICKNESS

Altitude sickness is real. The mildest form of acute mountain syndrome (AMS) is altitude sickness, caused when you ascend quickly to a height where there is less oxygen than what your body is accustomed to. Watch out for one or more of these symptoms:

- Headaches
- Loss of appetite
- Nausea
- Tiredness
- Trouble sleeping, and
- Dizziness.

If you find you are getting breathless without significant exertion, or confused over small things, you may be in danger of the fatal High–Altitude Pulmonary Edema (HAPE). The only remedy for that is to descend immediately.

Prevent AMS from destroying your trek by taking early action. The chief problem is the false belief that it is a sign of weakness to take any medication for altitude sickness. Altitude sickness has nothing to do with you, your fitness or your positive attitude. It is only about oxygen and how your body copes with lower levels of oxygen. If you have suffered from altitude sickness before, it will occur again.

For some people, altitude sickness can start at any height beyond 8000 feet or 2500 meters. At that height the early signs of mountain sickness: tiredness, shortness of breath and inability to sleep can begin. Diamox is the accepted treatment for altitude sickness. You need a prescription from your doctor for Diamox, and you must start this 24 hours before you ascend, and take it daily.

Other preventive steps are to drink a lot of water, ascend slowly, not more than 500 m a day, and rest between climbs. The ideal itinerary is to add rest days at Auli, Gobind Ghat, and Ghangaria, with another rest day before a second ascent to the Valley of Flowers, or Hemkund Sahib.

TRANSPORTATION

If you are heading into India for this trip, Delhi is the best choice of arrival. You can land at the International airport, catch the Metro to the Domestic Airport (a single stop away), and wait there for your flight to Dehradun. Flights to Dehradun start from 5:30 a.m.

You need to reach Gobind Ghat, the jump–off point of the trek, a tiny village on the road to Badrinath, from where a trekking path turns off the road to climb into the mountains. The road crosses an iron bridge over the river, and is motorable for four kilometers, before the trekking path begins. Gobind Ghat is in the valley of the Vishnu Ganga, just beyond the confluence where the Vishnu Ganga joins the Alaknanda.

Buses and Taxis to Auli via Joshimath are available from major destinations of Uttarakhand state like Rishikesh, Pauri, Rudraprayag, Karnaprayag, Ukhimath, Srinagar, and Chamoli.

A bus from Rishikesh to Badrinath leaves Rishikesh at 5:30 a.m., reaches Badrinath at 5:30 p.m., after passing Gobind Ghat and Joshimath.

There are plenty of shared taxis/jeeps, or you can hire one for your own use, either from Haridwar, or Joshimath. The latter is the recommended option.

The road is long, winding and steep, and traffic on it is subject to sudden stops, landslides and long army convoys. If you have any form of motion sickness, take motion sickness medicine, keep some ginger or Hajmola sweets handy.

If you get bad motion sickness, ask to sit in the front of the vehicle. If you flying in Dehra Dun, take the (unused) air-sickness bags with you off the plane.

FOOD

There are plenty of hot and hearty meals (and snacks) on the way, served with lashings of hot masala chai, or tea. Take precautions to eat food that is fully cooked, hot and fresh, and wash all fruit in bottled water before you eat it. Avoid all salads or raw cut vegetables and fruit, as you do not know how cleanly they have been prepared.

Dhabas or roadside food stalls serve basic Indian food on the route up to Ghangaria, and onto to Hemkund, and there's simple free food at the gurudwaras, at *guru ka langar*. Restaurants and stalls provide vegetarian Indian/Punjabi or even South Indian food in Ghangaria, and Gobind Ghat.

For the trek into the Valley of Flowers itself, you must carry your own food and water from Ghangaria. Carry water and force yourself to drink water along the way, however cold and wet it is, as dehydration at high altitudes can precipitate AMS.

Carry protein bars, nuts or trail–mix to supplement the food, as you may not feel hungry enough for a full meal, despite the delicious food available.

Avoid sitting in the restaurants, or be prepared to wait to allow for distancing. It is better to collect your food in your own containers, and eat it outside in an uncrowded place. Carry your own containers and cutlery and wash them your-self again before eating from them.

FEES AND RATES

You need to pay National Park fees to enter the valley, as well as other costs if you hire a porter or a mule.

The Forest Department checkpoint, less than a kilometer from center of Ghangaria is where you pay the fee to enter the Valley. Enter your name in a well–thumbed manuscript, and obtain your slightly grubby–looking permit. Make sure you carry appropriate photo ID, *Aadhar* card for Indians and passport for foreign nationals.

The fee to enter the Valley of Flowers, is 150 Rupees for Indians and 650 Rupees for foreigners for a 3–day pass. Each additional day is 250 Rupees for foreigners and 50 Rupees for Indians.

A guide can cost from 1000 to 2000 Rupees. Please do not haggle for their services, it is well worth paying for local knowledge, and remember that they have only a four–month season in which to earn a living.

Other fees fluctuate from day to day, you could pay 1,000 rupees upwards per person for a porter or a mule, for the trek into Ghangaria from Gobind Ghat. Hire a porter at the minimum to carry your backpack up – you are supporting the fragile Himalayans economy.

Travel by helicopter from Gobind Ghat to Ghangaria (or the opposite direction) costs about 3,500 rupees one way, per person for a person weighing up to 80 kilograms. More than that and you pay extra per kilogram. You can carry hand baggage of only four kilograms for the helicopter ride, you will have to send the rest of your luggage by porter or mule.

WHAT YOU SHOULD WEAR

You want to look good and be dry and comfortable.

- Water and wind–proof jacket (maybe with a separate warm jacket inside that can be worn alone if necessary). On some days you will need both, and on others one or the other. Ensure that these have plenty of pockets to stow away your phone, camera, some change and any small things that you don't want to open your backpack for. In fact, aim to never have to open your backpack while walking.
- A hidden travel belt under your clothes with your passports, credit cards, extra cash. Carry cash at all times, as the roadside stalls don't take credit cards.
- Light water–and wind–resistant walking trousers (though I have seen people wearing skirts, ski pants, sports tights). Make sure the size allows you to tuck your travel belt into it.
- An inner undershirt—either merino or lighter, NOT cotton.
- Several long–sleeved or short sleeved T–shirts suitable for the season, either light or merino again, OR a shirt of a material that wicks moisture away,

with pockets for safe stowage of your mobile phone and cash for the day.

- A fleece jacket, a size up from your usual size. This will enable you to wear an extra layer of whatever you have in case it gets chilly.
- A rainproof jacket that you can slip on over your jacket.
- A poncho is also a good choice. In fact, I recommend that you definitely use this, even if it is not raining, to protect your clothes from infections
- A belt for your water bottle, or you can carry this on the sides of your backpack
- Wear two pairs of socks with well laced up hiking shoes with tough soles, and add a rainproof cover for your backpack and day pack.
- A sunhat, and a warm hat, as you may need one or the other, or both.
- A long scarf, bandanna or *dupatta* to keep your throat warm, and to cover your head in temples or gurudwaras.
- A small day back to carry water, rain gear, and some food.
- Carry hand sanitizer, insect repellent, Vicks Vaporub, cough lozenges, and any medication that you would normally use.
- Mask, or disposable masks. Do not trek in these, but even fairly ordinary masks used when you are signing into your accomodation, or buying food can protect you. Take enough, so that you can change them frequently.
- Gloves, and disposable gloves. The normal gloves may be needed when at higher altitudes, but the disposable gloves are essential for when you are using

any public facilities such as toilets, restaurants, or shops.

WHERE TO STAY

The government-run Garhwal Mandal Vikas Nigam (GMVN) guesthouses provide reliable budget accommodation, and advance bookings are possible and recommended. There are other hotels and guesthouses as well. See Appendix B.

After the first day's drive, spend the night at Joshimath, Auli or Gobind Ghat before starting the trek to Ghangaria. The gurudwaras at Gobind Ghat and Ghangaria offer safe and clean accommodation, and free vegetarian food. There are also private rooms in both *gurudwaras* on payment if you don't wish to sleep in the *halls* or dormitories. Accommodation and food are available to all regardless of religion, caste or gender.

At Ghangaria you can find a range of accommodation from cheap guesthouses to "luxury" tents for glamping. Prices range from between 200 rupees to 3,000 rupees per night. Western style toilets and bathrooms are available, and of tolerable cleanliness. Wipe down every surface with disinfectant wipes, but do NOT flush the wipes. Place them in your waste bag and carry off the mountain.

Steps to upper levels can be open to the sky, slippery and dangerous, take care, or ask for a lower floor.

With tourist departments mandating new standards and rules for accomodation, it is best to be prepared to take your own bedding, sheets, and even pillows.

The cheaper guesthouses and backpacker hostels can be claustrophobic, lack views and have questionable standards of cleanliness. I would avoid these until the pandemic ends.

Electricity and water supply are erratic, and the only hot water is provided at extra charge by the bucketful. Ask the hotel attendant to leave it outside your room door, rather than carrying it into your bathroom.

Carry several sleeping bag liners, and your own sleeping bag and pillows.

Always get a hotel with insect screens, as despite the cold, the wet brings out monster mosquitoes. I spent an hour on the first evening, swatting the infiltrators individually, before the hotel boy kindly gave me a can of insect spray that blitzed the lot of them. These mosquitos were a centimeter long, black and persistent.

The solar powered lights come on after dusk for a few hours, so be ready to pack and unpack and leaving your room in a semi darkness.

Here's where camping and hiking discipline comes in handy. Line up your backpacks, trekking poles and shoes, and cover them if they are exposed to the elements, or other people.

Lock your accommodation with your own lock and key, to prevent any entry when you are away. Inform the staff that you are doing this.

Wipe down all surfaces, switches, handles, taps before you use them in your room, or bathroom.

BAGGAGE

Travel light. But not too light. If you are flying into India, or Dehradun, you will need check-in baggage for your trekking poles, warmer clothes and rain gear. See Appendix A.

If you have backpacks, you will need sturdy waterproof bags to place these into, for loading onto mules. You also need plastic bags to place over these to prevent infection in transit.

GETTING TO THE START OF THE VALLEY

The base for the trek to the Valley of the flowers is Ghangaria, a seasonal settlement. No ponies are allowed, and porters are not recommended.

The stages for the trek are:

- Ghangaria to Valley of Flowers check point – Upward slope of about half a kilometer. Checkpoint to Pushpavati river crossing – Gentle downslopes to boisterous river.
- Dwari Pairi to Baman Daur at Valley of Flowers – a steep and winding 1.5 kms, followed by a gentler climb of 2 kms.

TIME AT THE TOP

The trouble with Hemkund and Valley of Flowers is that you are confined to a short window of time, you must be off the mountain by 5 p.m., so that shrinks the amount of time you have at the top.

Plan to leave by 7 a.m., so that you can reach the Valley of Flowers by at least 10 a.m. This will give you time to walk further into the valley, an additional four to five kilometers reveals magic vistas with few crowds and more flowers. The walk down from the Valley can take up to three hours, and plan to start walking back by 2:00 p.m. or 3:00 p.m. at the very latest.

The way up to Hemkund is a wider formed path, but take care, the stones can be shaky and slippery, though the path is wider than the narrow path to the Valley of flowers, you still need to to take care, especially in the wet and slippery parts where the path cuts through the glacier.

Above the forests the sweeping mountain vistas make the long scramble to the top rewarding. Even on a rainy day, you will have patches of sunshine. This path is always populated by pilgrims, but for some reason, maybe the broadness of the path, or the number of teashops to stop and have a cup of tea, make it less crowded.

If you like a bit more space, avoid June, as at the start of the season is a time when the *gurudwara* opens after a long winter, is a busy time. The *gurudwaras* and hotels are likely to be packed with pilgrims, so ensure that you have confirmed bookings if you must come at this time.

The season ends in the first week of October, or the first snowfall which ever is earlier.

PART II

In Search of the Gods

CHAPTER 4
DEEP SOUTH TO FAR NORTH
EMANCIPATION

> *How many decades will there be before the Indian woman is emancipated from the mental, moral and physical slavery she has endured for countless generations?*

> — *Frank Smythe, The Valley of Flowers*

In the beginning there was a quiet valley, veiled in cloud and wreathed in glaciers and utterly remote from the teeming masses of the plains. But then one day it welcomed a lost wanderer stumbling out of a Himalayan storm, and it became known as the Valley of Flowers to the world.

The people of the mountain, the simple shepherds had long known this valley as *Nandan Kanan*, the last verdant valley before the brown dry hills of Tibet that lay in the rain shadow of the mighty Himalayas. And year after year it lay quiet and forgotten, except by a few intrepid souls ready to walk for days to reach it.

And when we knew of it, it was like a dream hovering in the distant north. In the vibrant south of India, we got on with converting the sleepy retirement town of Bangalore to the IT capital of the world, and building careers that as Indian women, not even our mothers could have dreamed of.

And we, answer Frank Smythe's question – a single generation. In 1937, when he wrote his book, my mother was a ten-year-old in a small town far in the south called Podanur, and on the trek in the photograph above, I stand in the exact spot where Frank Smythe asked that question.

AN IMPULSE TO ACTION

It starts as a conversation on Whatsapp across three continents – when were we going to do the things we wanted to do? With the people we wanted to do it with?

It was already June, and the monsoon was late, it gave us an opportunity – we could walk the Valley of Flowers in early August or September. One by one, we go over the options; independently, or hiring our own taxi, walking on our own, pre-booking? There was no guidebook that we could consult, so we throw our search net far and wide over the internet.

The options narrow as we realize we have limited time; we cannot wait around to catch buses or shared taxis, and I'm always car-sick on mountain roads. We need our own car and driver. And I need to sit in the front.

It later transpires that the roads are so precipitous and wet, and the curves so continuous and convoluted, that I sit one row back in the car, but that's another story.

Once we have our dates and times, it's time to plan. We have a ten-day window for a three-day trek, that sounds easy. Until we realize that we need to get to the valley, and acclimatize for the upper Himalayan heights. I have no qualms about admitting that I have altitude sickness, so we need a slow ascent to the start of the Valley of Flowers.

We hand over all the decisions to the best planner among us, Anju takes it all over, and we mostly nod and smile as she does a great job. I smile to myself as I think back to the time ages ago in an office far far away, I mistook her for someone's little sister, not a key developer on India's first supercomputer.

THE 10–DAY PLAN

This then was the 10–day plan:

Day One – from Dehradun airport to Kirtinagar.

Day Two – from Kirtinagar to Auli, a long and winding drive.

Day Three – A day's acclimatization at Auli with a trek to Gorson Top.

Day Four – Drive to Gobind Ghat and walk to Ghangaria.

Day Five – Walk into Valley of Flowers

Day Six – Walk into the Valley of Flowers

Day Seven – Walk to Hemkund Sahib

Day Eight – Walk back to Gobind Ghat. Drive to Auli via Badrinath and Mana.

Day Nine – Drive back to Haridwar

Day Ten – Drive to Jolly Grant airport and fly out.

And because of the monsoon, we factor in landslides and rain.

Many years ago, we had booked a rafting holiday in Rishikesh. On the drive up from Delhi a truck smashed into our car and sent us hurtling off the crossroads into a ditch full of murky water. Luckily, we had no major injuries, but that shook us up so much that we returned to Delhi and abandoned our rafting plan. Many decades later we rafted over the rapids as part of a white water expedition. But that road to Rishikesh always reminds me of that frantic drive and for years we couldn't eat *aloo paratha*, as that is what we were eating when that truck slammed into us and vanished into the dusty distance.

On this trip that ghost of *aloo paratha* would be laid to rest.

LOSING MY NOTES

At the long wait at Kuala Lumpur, I fill a notebook with ideas, then rush through security, sit down again and get the notebook out. My heart sinks, I scrabble through the bag. No book. Losing fresh written words – they're gone forever. No use crying over lost words.

In Delhi, it's an easy transit to the Domestic Terminal. Walk out, turn right and cross the road to the Metro station.

In the pre–dawn the bright lights were still blazing as we tumble into the packed terminal, and a wild wave above reveals Shanti, just in on a red eye flight from a business conference in Singapore.

At a certain age, you are averse to risk taking – and want to spend your precious holiday time with people who you know and like and trust. Pick your friends carefully in your youth. They are almost the only friends who will last the course.

We flee the dirty grey skies and murky clouds of Delhi and in half–an hour we glide over emerald hills threaded through with shining rivers as we come in to land at Dehra Dun.

The adventure begins.

CHAPTER 5

FOLLOWING THE GANGES

BELOVED RIVER

> The Ganga, is the river of India, beloved of her
> people, round which are intertwined her racial
> memories, her hopes and fears, her songs of triumph,
> her victories and her defeats.
>
> — *Jawaharlal Nehru*

The low green ridges and glinting streams vanish as we to come to rest at Jolly Grant airport. No one listens to the announcements as people leap up to grab bags, laptops and clothes from the overhead lockers. They're in a hurry to dash into the mountains. Who or what was Jolly Grant – that name makes me smile as we shake ourselves out of our seats and do an impromptu jig in the aisle – having eaten our second South Indian breakfast of the day, we need to move along.

Sleepless travel nights end in double breakfasts, and views of the Shivaliks, the low foothills of the mighty Himalayas. We venture into these today.

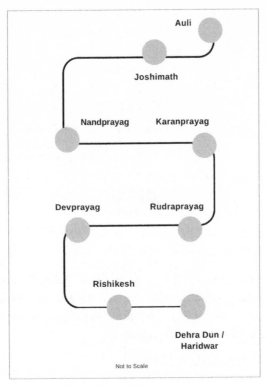

Auli

Joshimath

Nandprayag   Karanprayag

Devprayag   Rudraprayag

Rishikesh

Dehra Dun /
Haridwar

Not to Scale

Dehradun to Auli

Down the stairs, we stream over the warm tarmac into the small airport terminal, eager for our great adventure. Shanti and I head off purposefully towards the "Ladies", there will no more toilets for some time.

Outside a scream of cars and motor vehicles swoop past, stopping briefly to scoop up their targets – but ours is a few minutes away, and we stand about in the cool air laughing and talking and thinking of the trip. We descend back to giggles as a certain joy wells up – just a great sense of joy – is this what hundreds of sages have felt as they approach the mighty Himalayas?

Our taxi swerves into the gate and halts before us, with the early arrivals, Anju and Vibha waving at us. There can be little doubt that we are off on a girls own adventure.

JOLLY HAPPY CHAPPIE

I forget the lost notebook and any trepidations of the trek, with an airport called Jolly and a driver called Happy. This bodes well. Rain or no rain, this is not going to be anything but spectacular in this company.

We reflect modern India. Two North Indians who grew up in South India, and two South Indians who grew up in North India, all talking mostly English, at Indian speed of thought, and complete lack of personal space.

The luggage is stashed on the roof, wrapped up in tarps, as it can rain anytime. We head out, and Anju and Vibha pull out special Haridwar treats. And Shanti produces *parathas* and *chillas* from her bag. We will never starve in this company. I have visions of us tramping along the high Himalayas in a snowstorm, and then sitting down and pulling out our second breakfasts. I have my hobbit cape on the ready.

We fling off the dusty outskirts of Dehra Dun as we plunge into a finger of forest that Happy assures is the lair of bears and leopards. At Rishikesh, the last temple town, before the Ganges leaves the mountains forever, we push on and promise ourselves that we will attend *aarti* on the way back. In any case, Happy tells us, the Laxman Jhula footbridge over the Ganga is closed. Anticipation climbs over the day of temple visits and dips in the Ganges, as we brush up on our Hindi and mythology.

A HOW NOT TO DRIVE ON MOUNTAINS

Happy is a veritable fount of knowledge about temples and obscure myths, all recounted in chaste Hindi that sometimes foxes me. Bless ourselves with *Chintis*? Ants? That can't be right?

Here, a temple, a shrine! Stop! Go! The trek and the sacred merge into an indivisible feast, as I lean back and close my eyes, breathing in the rushing air, moist with a misty rain that hits the windscreen and vanishes into the churn of the windscreen wipers. Kirtinagar, our night halt, is not far, so we have time to linger along the way as Happy revels in sharing these mountains and its hidden and not-so-hidden shrines.

The road unspools ahead of us, and the curves climb higher and steeper. Happy whips the car along at speeds that take our breath away, are we going over the edge?

The highway will get worse soon, says Happy, so when we have the chance we should drive fast on the good roads.

Right, so we are heading fast into a week of slowing down.

A steady flow of cars, buses and trucks lumber on. At the side of the road, there is continuous work to hold back the rebellious mountainside. Vast baskets of wire and blocks of yellow shaded rock try to keep the mountain from collapsing onto the thin thread of road. I wonder if it will work, at times an unrestrained waterfall bursts down the steep cliffs and flows over the road in a defiant slick of muddy water.

Will we find a place that we can get down to the banks of the sacred river?

Through the green foothills, we pass narrow shanty towns racked with rusty tin roofs. At last, a place where we can walk down to the river and immerse our feet in the holy water of the Ganges. Ganges water is central to all blessing rituals, from birth to death. And treks, we would like this blessing before we walk.

SACRED FEET

At a closed–for–the–monsoon ashram, Happy pulls in and parks, leaving us to go down a twisting series of steps, passing the garishly painted ashram and the temple dozing in the late morning sun. The Ganges of course is never closed. A notice on suitable behavior warns us to dress and behave respectfully. We giggle looking at our oh so respectable clothes. Boots and all.

On the sandy riverbed studded with rounded boulders a tiny flock of butterflies congregate, they fly off in wave of minuscule wings, but settle back down a short way off. They're unafraid of us, bumbling giants.

A newly built concrete temple overlooks the churning waters as the Ganges sweeps around the foot of a green hillock. Yes, the hills are still low here, we are in the Shivaliks, the foothills. We skip, hop and even dance down to the water, strip off shoes and socks to immerse our feet in the ice–cold water, first the toes, then the sole and finally the heel. I shiver with the sudden cold for a minute before we splash into the river, spreading out our arms to balance between the rocks and pebbles on the riverbed. We look like we're doing an ungainly bird dance, except for the danseuse, Vibha who breaks into fluent Kathak.

Magical myth, history and reality, collide here as we dip our feet and paddle in the swift–flowing water that pushes against us. Childhood picnics to various rivers and lakes flash back in full color and sound. With our mothers warning us of the dangers of deceptive currents that can carry us away. We tread carefully but not fearfully, we are the mothers now, and we've left our children behind. Is this the real feeling of freedom then?

There is no doubt that the adventure has begun – and like our ancestors, rather than visiting a temple or a cathedral, we are here feet in the river, in a prayer to the mountains. Are we accessing the collective imaginations of a subcontinent and beyond. Is it the mountains themselves that are the heavens or gods? Can mere lumps of rock and ice fill us with such awe?

I wiggle my feet in the sand beneath the water and the water washes over my sandy toes. It may be muddy here but it's run-off, not dirt. It's too early for the Ganga to be full of crocodiles, human remains or the trash of half a billion people.

In this place she is still the sparkling stream running off the dreadlocked plait of blue necked Shiva. In this area is the Chota Char Dham, the four temples sacred to the myths: the muscularity of Kedarnath and Badrinath, and flowing softness of Gangotri and Yamunotri, a perfect balance of Yin and Yang.

THE CAVE SPIRIT

The dark face of a cave peers at us through the hanging creepers of the riverbank. Drawn to it we tiptoe over the rocks and boulders of the rocky beach, stooping onto the sandy–floored abode of a hermit, long gone. A splash of red paint and a dried garland of marigold and jasmine adorn a now forlorn sacred rock.

This is not the place for us, as yet, maybe in some other life we can take *sanyas* and come and live and meditate here – but this is too low, the hills are mere mounds. Ahead of us the eternal snows of the Himalayas are hidden in the boiling clouds of the monsoon. And our valley awaits us.

On another spiritual note, we have also stopped at Tapovan, not for the temple but for the "English" Liquor Shop, where we stock up on another kind of spirits. Just in case.

CHAPTER 6
THE COLOR OF WATER
STREAMS FROM HEAVEN

> *She has been a symbol of India's age–long culture and civilization, ever–changing, ever–flowing, and yet ever the same Ganga.*

— *Jawaharlal Nehru*

It wasn't the sinuous curves on the road that were making me hold my breath. Around every curve could appear that magic moment where geography and myth collide – the confluence of the ardent Alaknanda and the blissful Bhagirathi, the point at which the two seminal streams become the Ganga, the marriage of heaven and earth.

Round a curve and dripping down the hillside, Devprayag steps down to the bathing ghats at the edge of a peaked temple. Happy evicts us, and instructs us to descend, sprinkle Ganges water over our heads and clamber up a covered ramp to the road on the opposite side of the valley. We're not used to these brusque commands to holiness, but the dancing confluence below draws us down into a sacred vortex.

The downhill path transforms into a rocky stairway as we sidle between homes so close that we can see what's bubbling on the kitchen stove. Ahead the suspension footbridge over the river–filled gorge waits for that first tentative step. The long bridge dangles over the gorge, and from the other side a jangling cow swishes her tail as she clumps on over, and a man manhandles his moped onto it. Can the bridge take all of us? Blue strips of the icy Bhagirathi frame my stilled foot as I clutch the swaying side rail.

The cow lumbers past, secure in its sacred entitlement, and the moped man pushes his vehicle by, the whiff of diesel despoils the fresh mountain air – worse than the odor of the cow. The bridge sways as we move from side to side to get the best photos and then it's down the broken concrete steps to the *prayag*, or confluence.

DANCING ON THE GANGES

For such a significant spot it is empty of pilgrims – only the temple touts promising eternity and more. Tempting as it is to lift our heads and drink in the vistas, we keep our eyes glued to the uneven stone flagged steps until on the last platform, both rivers swirl over the rocks. Into the confluence, clinging to the rail. Holy feet but cold toes – I clench my toes gripping the rock as the water laps up over my ankles. Getting swept into the boiling rapids is not on my agenda, at least, not without a raft.

The blue Bhagirathi and the muddy Alaknanda create a two–color strip of moving water spreading downriver for half a kilometer or more. The ice–blue Bhagirathi, coming from the frigid Gangotri glacier, inches along, scorning the wild muddy dance of the boisterous Alaknanda. Coming off the high mountains, and tumbled into by countless valleys and rocks, the Alaknanda roars into the confluence, all power, noise, and mud.

Vibha translates this into Kathak as her flowing hand movements tell the story of the confluence in dance. It is real here, and so is the dance. In this moment loud with the roaring river, wet with the icy water, my thoughts still to nothingness.

A mountain breeze whisks down the valley, washes the tiredness from our faces, tosses our hair about, turning us into a wilder type of woman. We're ready to face anything the world can throw at us – except perhaps a cow on suspension bridge. But for now, we dance, laughing as Vibha moves our awkward limbs into graceful poses. We feel like goddesses dancing, with dirty feet.

On the return journey, we will meet the same river gliding sedately along at Haridwar, festooned with bright temples tinkling with brass bells, and flickering with a thousand lamps of glowing wicks dipped in ghee. But here, she is a wild young woman leaping off the mountain in a hurry to get to her destiny as the life giver of the northern plains of India.

Is that us too? The four of us, reinventing ourselves in our late prime. At our age, our mothers, sat down with knitting and grandchildren on the knees. We are pushing those same knees to climb mountains, and invent some goddesses for ourselves.

The ramp up to the road looked daunting from across the hill, here on the actual path, it's just one step after another. Happy and the car await us at the road, and we settle in and continue on our ever upward journey following the banks of the Alaknanda. We fed our souls, now it's time for food.

A CLIFF-HANGER OF A LUNCH

The road to Joshimath is magical, even the *dhabas* hover in thin air over the plunging cliffs. Parking on a tiny sliver of flat ground, we stop for lunch at a *dhaba* with no name and a river view. Through the grimy windows are ploughed fields edged by the glinting waters, and a set of rickety stairs tempt us up onto the roof. No railings or protection from the gusty wind, nothing but air separates us from a rural Himalayan scene, with a boiling river and opposite us a single hillock rises above a sandy white river beach.

Climbing down carefully, we sit at folding tables outside, to sip the spicy ginger tea and munch on crispy onion pakoras, the first of many such meals and snacks.

Kirtinagar, our night halt approaches, it is still daylight and we visit more temples. Happy is indefatigable in his visiting of temples, it seems a personal challenge that we visit every temple on the way. Nestled in groves and tucked in among boulders on the riverside, quiet shrines flutter flags with a single lamp burning in the dusk.

And then the rain rushes down on us. There will be no more temple visiting for the day. Happy concedes defeat and drives us to the hotel at Kirtinagar where we experience for the first time sets of interminable wet stairs tacked onto outer walls of buildings.

DANCING BY THE ALAKNANDA

Pushing open the creaking doors to the balcony lets the musty air out and the soft Himalayan air in. The Alaknanda roars beneath, flanked by a green lawn, on which two mountain ponies graze, swishing their tails, and blinking large lashes against the rain. Their bells tinkle through the rain and the roar. The rain thins to a drizzle, and we troop down to the river terrace, where Vibha leads us in a dance meditation – my dance moves need significant correction, but the meditation and stretching helps after the long hours crumpled in the car.

Then it's time for the evening meal, *palak paneer* and the piping hot *aloo parathas*, with a mix of pickles and fragrant *masala* tea. The manager assures us that there will be early breakfast and tea for us in the morning complete with more *aloo parathas*.

The whirling vortex of the day stills. Last night I was on a plane over the Bay of Bengal, tonight I'm sleeping by a river and on the edge of an adventure. The sound of Himalayan rain blunts the sound of the torrent that fills the slumbering valley.

We will follow the course of the Alaknanda all the way up to Gobind Ghat. I think of the explorer, Frank Smythe, headed up these verdant valleys, walking all the way with his entourage of porters and ponies. We have Happy, and a jeep piled high with backpacks. There are roads now, I feel some regret at the speed at which we will whirl past the many valleys and the innumerable hikeable tracks that we miss. Speed equals loss.

I plan to subvert Happy–ji's compulsory temple visiting plan tomorrow. The mountains are cathedrals enough for me.

The rain falls in gusty sheets that rattle the windows and peeking out between the velvet curtains, I note that the ponies have gone, and we sleep. Tomorrow we will reach Auli for a day and night of acclimatization before we push on to the Valley of Flowers.

CHAPTER 7
I LIFT MY EYES TO THE MOUNTAIN
VISION

> *As the dew is dried up by the morning sun, so are the sins of mankind by the sight of the Himalayas.*

—*Skanda Purana*

The spluttering of rain on the roof is one of my favorite sounds to wake up to, gulp hot tea and snuggle back to sleep. But not today. It's day two, and the adventure has begun. Yesterday we arrived at the foothills, and it begins to sink in, after the weeks of planning and preparation, we're here and on our way.

Kirtinagar skulks in the low hills – today we abandon it to its grey anonymity.

Dodging the rain, we descend the trippable multi staircases to the dining room for tea and breakfast. It's toast and fruit for me. That's better for a day with a long hilly drive. Happy assures us that he will take us to a great place for lunch, with a view. And excellent shudh "pure" vegetarian food. I glance away so he doesn't see my teenager worthy eye–roll.

Every roadside shack has a wonderful view on this path to paradise. It's a long uphill drive today to Auli and we have multiple confluences or prayags, each with a temple that we will have to visit.

The first town is Srinagar, the capital of the Garhwal region, not the one in Kashmir, though it is said that a sage from here visited Kashmir and founded that city. A large city along a wide valley, it clings to the mountains, but the river has been known to burst it banks and wash homes and farms away, so homes near the river live dangerously. In fact, the flood of 1894, utterly destroyed the old town. We pass through the "new" town, rebuilt in 1901, with Happy determined that we stop at our first temple, a women's temple to a Himalayan goddess.

THE MAROONED GODDESS

Dhari Devi – the women's shrine is set in the middle of a roaring torrent. It's raining, but that's no excuse, we head down to the temple accessed only by a walkway and wonder how people visited here before this bridge existed. Did they swim out clutching desperately to mud pots, did they take boats that battled the swirling waters that threatened to suck them down to a watery grave?

The covered walkway allows us to flip back our hoods to feel the breeze in our hair, and raising our hands we tinkle the myriad brass bells that festoon – both sides of the walkway, announcing our presence to the goddess Dhari Devi. It's a women's shrine, rare in the Himalayas, so we head into it for privileged blessings, and after that out again to cross the suspension bridge to the village at the other side.

All is silent in the shrine, where a single wall of bedrock marks the spot of the original ancient temple. We tramp around the rock in our cold bare feet. It may not be Kailash, but we've done one circumnavigation.

A rusted door bangs intermittently on a derelict cable car dangling midway over the torrent on a twisted wire rope. A relic of the 2013 floods that smashed down this valley, ripping out all the bridges, concrete footings and all. They called the army out for a huge search and rescue operation, and later they installed these cable cars to allow villagers to venture across the river, thereby also ruining the impromptu holidays of scores of rained in children.

A mist floats on top of the river even now, late in the morning, as the river thunders around the curve. In the roar is the creak of the rope and the dull thumps from the cable car, and I strain to hear the still small voice of the Spirit that created this mysterious web of water and earth, and brought me here to create this perfect moment.

A TRILOGY OF PRAYAGS

The Panch Prayag, the five confluences of the Alaknanda flow thick and fast, all aflutter with temple flags. Yesterday we passed Devprayag, and today we will pass three more. This route is the perfect Ganges worship, she who has no temples dedicated to her, but who gives life to the land and its myriad peoples.

We danced at Devprayag, but Rudraprayag is the abode of the music that impels our feet to tap and stomp and break into dance. Dance is divine, and here we are headed into the realms of the Hindu Lord of the Dance, Shiva. The temple here is in honor of Shiva in his dimension of Rudra, the god of music.[1]

At Rudraprayag the temples and river march straight down to the confluence of the Mandakini and the Alaknanda. Chamunda, the wife of Rudra also has her temple here at the prayag in perfect harmony of male and female.

Beyond the mountains start to raise their prodigious heads and peering over the edge strikes fear as the valley sides drop to faraway streams. Buses haul past us when we stop for photographs, alarming us with the rattle and wheeze of ancient brakes.

We stop at the only Krishna temple on the route, a tiny brightly colored shrine perched at the confluence of the Pindar and the Alaknanda at Karnaprayag, another of the sacred confluences or prayags. After we visit the tiny temple perched on a platform beneath large banyan trees, we stroll down to the quieter confluence.

A few more kilometers on roads where occasionally we inch past landslides where the edge of the road has melded into mush, we come upon Nandprayag and the first road sign for the Valley of Flowers.

At Nandprayag the Mandakini, proceeding from the pristine heights of Nanda Devi, and the Alaknanda meet at a boulder strewn confluence. No wonder the Alaknanda is so full and muddy at Devprayag – it's swallowing up whole rivers in its wake before arriving.

Instead of the temple, we stop at a hotel with a huge map painted on the wall, and in an open pavilion on the riverside with views of the temple, we eat a delicious meal off shining stainless *thalis*, or plates.

As we ready to leave, the car pulls over, and round the bend roars a long heavily laden army convoy. I recognize the signage on the convoy and a sudden bout of homesickness grips me.

FIRST VIEWS OF THE SNOWS

We whirl through Chamoli, only stopping to take pictures of the road signs that we see for Joshimath and Gobind Ghat. The reality of places that were mere dots on maps, send a thrill through me, and my friends laugh at the peculiar things that excite me. I wonder at the early explorers tracking through these paths and woods with only the peaks and stars to navigate by.

At Pipalkoti, in the cleft of the valley, we see it, the snow peaks of the Himalayas at last, wreathed in clouds, but unmistakable in their glow as they float across the sky. We stop and lift our eyes to the far horizon. The twisted crossing is filthy and rubbish–strewn, but look up for the view.

This is special, and soon we stop again at Garur Ganga, hunting for special stones in the pebbled riverbed below the temple after making our offering. A stone to protect our home from snakes of all kinds.

From here on the chatter quietens, as the road narrows and the gears grind for the serious climb towards to our final stop for the day. The road is steep, and the valleys plunge into infinity. Peeking over the side, the road below is a tiny thread that switches back in infinite loops above an invisible stream that gleams when vagrant rays of sunlight make it to the valley floor.

The mountains are like jagged teeth, raw sharp peaks that saw across the silver blue sky, and black rock slopes drop in vertical falls to unseen gorges below. Hathi Parbat and Gauri Parbat hide behind white clouds, teasing us with rare glimpses.

MAGICAL AULI

Perched high above the confluence of the Alaknanda and the Dhauli, Joshimath is ensconced in a circular depression, its protected position made it the winter retreat of the priests from Badrinath. A vital stop for pilgrims, it's original stone temples and buildings are scarred by the plague of modern concrete buildings.

We are now in the embrace of the high mountains, on the way we pass a power station, locked up and mute except for the hum of the wires. And then the raucous clamour of the marketplace, where we tumble out relieved to stretch our bodies and search for elusive ATMs.

These the last ATMs on the route, and we will need cash from now on, so we must find them. This is also the place for those last-minute purchases. We buy phone covers, as it rains incessantly, fleecy jackets and bright bandannas for our heads.

In winter a cableway allows day access to the ski slopes of Auli, but for us, we take the road. The increasingly steep roads climb to Auli, through apple orchards heavy with fruit, passing army cantonments, and later school buses packed with smartly dressed schoolkids – another reminder of army days. Joshimath and the Valley of Flowers are close to the Indo Tibetan border here, and the army is on constant alert.

At last the road ends, literally. Up steep flights of stairs with broken treads, pay attention as the steps are of irregular heights. Later we meet a group of retired professors, and while they are sprightly, I wonder how they managed the stairs, but the secret is out. There is another approach. You can drive up to the cable car station and then walk down a short set of stairs to the resort.

But for now, the "boys" from the resort come down and carry our bags up to the log cabins with the most magnificent views of the Himalayas. Even the late afternoon clouds and mist cannot fully obscure the jagged pyramids of sloping rock topped with snow peaks. From Kamet, to Neelkanth to Nanda Devi, all the abundance of peaks leaves us silent.

The view draws us out from the rooms, and we'd like to meet the other people here. The camp is packed with trekkers, and many of them seem to be from Bangalore. We meet people who have common acquaintances. At dinner we meet the owners, operators and guides. It's a sociable time.

It's also time to mix up and divide the trail mix, into multiple zip lock bags that we tuck into our baggage. We distribute our rations of protein bars, nuts and Hajmola sweets, and begin sorting through our shared tubes of Vaseline, Boroline, Vicks, insect repellent and sunscreen.

It is camp time definitely; as we need to wait for the hot water boilers to be fired up, and in the cabins the weak lights and charging points betray their solar origins. But we have lights – and the phones and other equipment charge, unlike earlier explorers, who used flickering candles or lanterns that spluttered in the wind.

At dusk, the camp is wreathed in a ghostly mist, but later in the night the mist clears and before us like magnificent ships of the night the mountains float in the moonlight. The Neelagiri massif sits astride the horizon, and to it's right, Gauri Parbat and Hathi Parbat hover in the distance, while closer to us Dunagiri raises a toothed spear to the sky.

SUSAN JAGANNATH

There is a little snow on the peaks, but what a wonder it would be in the winter when clearer nights and more snow would create a winter wonderland. The wide windows of the cabins look out on the view, framing them like a giant TV screen. But we are really here, not simply watching it on the television. And tomorrow more views and the first trek with flowers awaits us.

CHAPTER 8
EYE TO EYE WITH GIANTS
SUDDEN REVELATIONS

> *As we came out of the upper forest onto a wide alp.*
> *The clouds parted, revealing the great massif of*
> *Gauri Parbat and Hathi Parbat, and almost before I*
> *had time to take in the grandeur of this sudden*
> *revelation, a terrific icy spire, shining and*
> *immeasurably remote, thrust itself through the clouds,*
> *Dunagiri.*

Frank Smythe, The Valley of Flowers

Rain again, in the darkness after moonset, fat drops whip across the windows, in the Himalayas the rain can be horizontal. The day dawns early, but the high peaks mean that the only visible sunrise is a faint rose blush on the far mountains. The rain washes all the moisture out to reveal the views from 5 a.m., range after range, black and snowy, from dark jagged peaks to soft snow flurries stretch to the far horizons all the way to Tibet.

TO THE MEADOW

Gorson Top trail is our treat of the day, a short six–kilometer return hike through a Himalayan pine *chir* forest and up to the alpine meadows of Gorson *bugyal*. Today we will meet our Valley of Flowers guide, sign disclaimers, plan the trek, and learn what to expect.

But for now, it's out to trek to the meadow. We saunter out past log cabins and rooms with mountain views, clamber up yet more stairs and come to the cable car station. I tilt my head, shading my eyes, and on impulse decide to ride the cable car for a five–minute ride to the lake. The grey bearded guard clanks the safety rail down over me and I forget my vertigo, as we glide upwards on the metal wire of the ropeway. Beneath us trekkers are plodding along, dodging cowpats and rocky outcrops. Then it's off and through some slushy paths to the lake.

I'm suspicious of the brown churned up slush, as there are a lot of cows here, so I inch along on narrow grassy verges. The artificial lake enclosed with a wire fence against the ever–present cows, services the slopes with plumes of snow in winter, for Auli is one of India's few ski slopes. A bench by the lake lets me admire the massive ski lodge, and café on the slope above the lake. It sits shuttered and silent in green meadows covered with flowers, and grazing cows.

Still higher on the slope is another grey glassed in cable station, where Asia's highest cable car ropeway connects the slopes with Joshimath, a four–kilometer ride. The pillars and cables vanish downhill out of sight. Feeling brave after my short cable car ride, I resolve to come back one winter. I forget my resolution not to repeat places.

Arms interlinked, in baggy salwars and slippers, a young couple from Switzerland gaze all around them. The mountains are taller and more magnificent, and more abundant, they gesture at the ring of giants, now wreathed in torn rips of blown cloud. An abundance of mountains, that's a new collective for the Himalayas.

The names of the soaring peaks are the stuff of legend. In a vista from Neelkanth to Nanda Devi, one enormous massif after another rears its rocky snow flecked head in a majestic march across a blindingly blue Himalayan horizon. Not just home of the snows, Home of the Gods indeed. It is no wonder that Adi Shankaracharya seized upon this area to re-animate a fading Hinduism from the push of an austere and logical Buddhism. The Indian soul loves stories, and there are none better than those set in these divine mountains. We salute him, does he salute us back, four women from his home in the deep south, a thousand years apart?

THE BELLOWING BULL

The climb and the cable car ride have made my throat dry and raspy. The water trickles down my throat as the forest at the edge of the meadow approaches. Also, my nemesis–did I mention that I fear bovines? Do you know that cows kill more people per year than hippopotamuses? This titbit of trivia rushes back as a shaggy black and white bull rushes to the edge of his field and bellows. It shakes his massive head, and his wicked red eyes glare at me. Dear God, if I have to die in the Himalayas, let it not be in this undignified way—a Yeti, ok, but not a cow!

Then a family of grandmother, mother, daughter lope up behind us, herding along a baby calf and mother cow. The fluffy black calf was born in the lower meadow, and the women have come down from their summer grazing ground to take mother and calf to the lush meadows above. Their summer village is two kilometers away in the alpine meadows at the top of the rise.

The wobbly calf blinks and nuzzles the elbow of the old woman, who is carrying her like a human baby. The bull trails along the wall, snorting and bellowing, until the wall ends, and he can no longer walk alongside. I hear his anguished mooing for a long time as we climb up towards the forest. A bull is a protective Dad, too.

The three villagers are the same as a family anywhere, the teenager is doing no work and giving lip to her grandmother and mother, and the mother is looking pained, and the grand-mother is laughing and carrying the calf – the oldest but she is doing the most and hardest work. They walk along with us, happy to pose for photos and chat – though the chatting is limited as none of us can speak Garhwali, but warm smiles and laughing eyes are enough.

A tiny breeze trembles through the heavy conifer branches, the light is a filtered green, and the rocks alongside the path are soft with velvety moss. The trio of nimble village women leap up to shake down the hanging lichens and pick up sheaves of dry moss, stuffing them into bags as they overtake us, cow, calf and all. They distill indigenous medicine from the moss and lichen, natural antibiotics they tell us.

ENCOUNTERING HANUMAN

The fallen leaves and bright green patches of moss make the forest slippery underfoot, but the tall trees shade us and soon we shrug ourselves back into our discarded jackets. The tall pines stand thick and still, with strands of silvery lichen dangling down, and a resinous scent filling the air.

Ahead, a lick of faint saffron quivers through the trees, a sign of a temple or shrine. And sure enough, in the distance, some other trekkers perch on a low stone wall sipping from their water bottles, talking to a pujari, or temple priest. By the time we arrive they have vanished into the dark forest, and the pujari turns around from the idol to see if we want a blessing or a puja. It's dedicated to Hanuman, the monkey god, how appropriate here in the forest.

Dark-skinned compared to the mountain peoples, with a saffron lungi draped on his narrow hips, with long well shampooed hair in an elegant man bun, he is barefoot on the cold stones that pave the tiny courtyard before the shrine. I wonder at how his feet are so clean, can he fly? Is he Hanuman himself perhaps? But alas, no sign of a tail. Still this is the home of the Gods, so maybe they do walk among us.

A feast of flags of various shapes and sizes and color flutter on the faint mountain breezes. We rest awhile in the forecourt of the miniscule Hanuman shrine before the last push to the meadow on the top of the mountain.

MEETING FRANK IN THE MEADOW

Out onto the meadow, we blink in the sudden light as the sun strikes us sharp and clear, and we flop down on the grass, amidst bunches of flowers, like living bouquets, white and blue anemones, daisies and mountain marigold. Then we scale some rocks and a rolling vista of flower studded meadows unfolds. In the distance the toiling figures of the three women, the cow and the calf fade into the mist like fantasy figures from a myth, and even the tinkle of the cowbells disappears.

It's time for our packed lunch, we nibble on the tasteless biriyani, and look back down to Auli and we are eye to eye with giants. The spoon drops to the ground, the food forgotten.

The clouds have vanished, and the vast range dominates the horizon beneath a brilliant blue sky. From Neelkanth, Kamet, Neelagiri, Hathi, Gauri Parbat and on to Dunagiri, are all so close it seems we could touch them – except for the dizzying chasms between us. Only Nanda Devi sheathes herself in mist. The goddess is still hiding herself.

This is where we intersect with the route Frank Smythe took from Ranikhet to Joshimath, crossing the Kuari Pass to emerge onto this meadow. A thrill runs through me as our story and his merge on this shining meadow with views of heaven.

" As we came out of the upper forest onto a wide alp. The clouds parted, revealing the great massif of Gauri Parbat and Hathi Parbat, and almost before I had time to take in the grandeur of this sudden revelation, a terrific icy spire, shining and immeasurably remote, thrust itself through the clouds, Dunagiri".

And, earlier in the morning we met the three mountain women, confident and calm, compared to the frightened small woman he met. Reading the chapter in his book, it seems likely that this is the same slope. But what a difference the 90 years have made.

".. a small woman driving some oxen appeared. She seemed terrified when I questioned her and hastened by with averted eyes."

It's monsoon, there is less snow. The inky black rock peaks are streaked with white glaciers, the jagged profile like the teeth of a vampire saw at the fragile sky. Thin fir forests cover some slopes, but most are sheer falls of gleaming black rock.

Tomorrow we will head into them and climb even higher than today. The guide points out where the Valley of Flowers nestles beneath Kamet and Neelagiri. We strain our eyes to see it. It seems impossibly high and impossibly far. I wonder if it was better to walk there and slowly ascend in the manner of pilgrims of old.

A SLIPPERY SOUL

As we trek back to Auli, the mists close in around us in a damp obscuring embrace. The wet leaves and soft moss give way under my boot, and despite digging my trekking pole in, I swerve to avoid the rocks and it's into the mud. In another slippery episode, Shanti loses her sole (of her old boot) and Vibha slips to inflame an old knee injury. It's a limping race to the cabins.

Back at the camp, we revel in the spectacular views as we sip tea in front of our log cabins. Nothing is grander than this. The sun disappears suddenly, plunging us in darkness. Indoors it is, and we dig out the glue and use a lace to lash the sole to the shoe and wonder if we can find a mochi in Auli or Joshimath.

At moonrise a wash of mountain scape captures us while we sip more hot tea, but the lure of hot baths drags us indoors, hot water being available only for half an hour.

Later we meet our guide, get his firm instructions to be ready to leave at 7 a.m. and prepare our trekking gear. We need to travel light but not too light. Because it is monsoon, clothes won't dry, so we take multiple t-shirts, walking shorts or tights and jackets. We're are escaping the household chores. That's my constant dream.

PART III

Finding the Goddess

CHAPTER 9
BOOTS ON THE GROUND
PORTERS, PONIES AND PALANQUINS

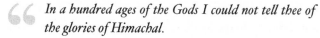

In a hundred ages of the Gods I could not tell thee of the glories of Himachal.

– Sage

Out of the snug beds at 5 a.m., it's a rush of stuffing backpacks and labelling baggage. On go all the layers, like good hikers we are prepared to peel on or peel off layers, depending on the weather. Today's the first day of a long trek, on goes the Vicks Vaporub on my feet, followed by the two pairs of socks, and then the boots, laced up correctly. Check – Raingear is handy, and water bottles are ready for filling, snacks and trail mix accessible?

On the guide's orders, like good soldiers, we are prepped and ready by 6:30 a.m. We dodge the early rain, making a beeline for breakfast. But, no one told the camp kitchen that we needed early tea and breakfast, so despite the early rising, there is no 7 a.m. departure. The kitchen hut is silent, no smoke billows out of the chimneys and long lumpy sleeping bags move slightly on the kitchen floor when we shout out "Good morning"!

We sit around, tapping our heels and pressing our lips together to prevent grumbling in this spectacular location.

TROUBLE IN PARADISE

This is a serious annoyance and it rapidly worsens. We expect basic services, if this camp is only for trekkers to the Valley of Flowers only, don't they know that the guides want us to be on our way early?

But we have time to take more photos, as in the early morning nothing obscures the face of the mountain. Breakfast is even later than usual, and even after that, we wait until we find out why. It seems there is a war of pettiness between the kitchen staff and cleaners and the guides, and we get caught in the middle. Maybe Lean, or Agile methodology could work here – a seminar on "Start with Why", but we push those thoughts away, it is far too much like work.

The story unfolds grudgingly, the other small group that should have joined us arrived late at night and slept in, and then, their payment does not go through. Not a surprise, seeing that internet access at Auli was less than stellar. The guide dismisses us, urging us to join another large group of 20 strangers. Don't get me wrong, we're ready to be flexible, but not be pushed around. Don't mess with us because we are women – we object and refuse to back down until the owner steps in to resolve the issue.

Not a good start, marking an uneasy relationship with the tour guide. Given that we had paid a lot of money each, this was poor service and we were not ready to suck it up. It mars the start of a magical trek, so do consider the wisdom of putting all your eggs in one basket. With excellent hindsight, it is not too hard to arrange this trek on your own, because despite the "end–to–end" nature of the tour we had purchased, there were irritants, like a pebble in your boot.

We set off past 10 a.m., with no time to stop on the way (for more of Happy's temples), reach Gobind Ghat, and then walk the 11 kilometers up to Ghangaria. But we have to fix Shanti's shoe. At Joshimath an old–school mochi hunched over his awl at the side of the road, repairs the boot. He mentions that his sons manage the two posh shoe shops opposite him. He is the last generation of roadside mochis, once ubiquitous in any town in India. Was this progress? Maybe, maybe not. Sole safely reattached with glue and neat stitching, we're on our way.

THE ALAKNANDA GORGE

On the brief drive downhill from Joshimath, the sides of an ever younger Alaknanda press in on us. Happy scowls that we will miss the temple at Vishnuprayag. For once I agree as we whizz by, this prayag is the wildest, the flung spray showering the temple with icy water. Plunging through vertical gorges, this is where the Vishnu Ganga meets the tumultuous Alaknanda, the first, or last of the Panch Prayags of the Alaknanda. The gorge walls are nearly perpendicular, and the Vishnu Ganga is as riotous as the Alaknanda. We are still on the ancient pilgrim trail to Badrinath, in the footsteps of millions of pilgrims from ages past and all over India.

We pull into Gobind Ghat, before the bridge, where a huge elevated road sign points the way to the Valley of Flowers as a dotted trail. As we leave the taxi, Happy promises to pick us up from the same place when we get back in a few days. He reminds us that Gobind Ghat is another place where you can buy gear that you may have forgotten for the trek, cheap rain gear, used shoes, and stout walking sticks, and locally grown apples, other fruit and water.

A cacophony blasts us as we leave the safety of Happy's taxi. *Ponywallah* or muleteers crowd us in, offering mules, luggage services and general chaos. The guide stands apart and refuses to help, leaving us to negotiate the melee as best we can. The argument is that the tour operators could not know the price on the day – an irritant that annoys when you have picked an operator who claims to know and do everything. Or maybe he was just furious at our altercations earlier in the day.

The sky buzzes, and a helicopter comes whirring low over our heads descending rapidly to the helipad below the gurudwara, about half a kilometer down the road towards Badrinath. They buzz up and down the valley between 9 a.m. to 4 p.m., in the season, weather permitting. However, the wait can be a few hours. But it is a four-minute ride, compared to a four to five-hour walk.

But no helicopter for us, we're here to walk.

We cram into a packed share jeep, cross the suspension bridge, and head off to Pulna the road-head. We waved at trekkers walking up the road. The four kilometer walk from Pulna does not tempt us, a tarred road with lots of traffic, and little or no shade all the way to Pulna. If you do wish to walk all the way, give yourself enough time, as it is a steep hike with uncertain weather. Rain and mist can complicate the trek and you must reach Ghangaria before night fall, so walking from Gobind Ghat is only for the fast and fit.

PRESSING ON FROM PULNA

From the shop lined street at Pulna, the stone–lined path shaded with Himalayan oak and rhododendron climbs around the first curve. The path runs all along the valley side, beneath us to the right, the Bhyundar Ganga rushes down to meet the Alaknanda.

But first we negotiate luggage rates with the muleteers, load up the mules[1], or hire a porter to carry your daypack. Why not? This is also the place to hire animal or human transport for the trek. Mules, porters and palkis are all available.

You can hire a *pittoowallah*, or porter to carry you all the way – you sit backwards in a basket that the porter hefts onto his back and off you go. This can be nerve–wracking, but hold your nerve and do not move in the basket.

And there is is the palki option, where like days of old you sit in a seat and four porters bear you aloft, balancing the poles on their shoulders.

After a quick stop for tea and fortifying snacks, we sidle past a herd of tethered mules, avoiding the steaming heaps of dung, and the wrong end of a mule. Notice how it keeps it left leg on tiptoe? This is not an elegant pose for Instagram, this is to get in a swift kick to anyone coming too close. The backward kick of a mule can break bones and put a painful end to your trek. I know this as a military brat who grew up around animal transport companies. The "ponies" are in fact mules, or *Khachads*. A mule is the offspring of a male donkey and a mare, and is an artificial infertile breed created by humans. These civilian mules in Pulna are no match for the handsome, strong mules bred for the Army. And they always have female names, *Shobha*, *Rani* and *Devi* are common names I heard yelled out by the muleteers.

India's Prevention of Cruelty to Draught and Pack Animals Rules, 1965, says the maximum load for mules is 200 kilograms, however the US Army specifies a maximum of 20 percent of body weight for mules walking up to 20 miles a day in mountains, giving a load of up to about 200 pounds or 91 kg. The mules here carry less than 100 kgs of weight, so animal–lovers need not stress.[2]

If you have any doubts about your ability to walk 11 kilometers uphill, hire a mule. The mules are sure–footed and intelligent, their stubbornness makes them refuse to put their lives (and yours) in danger. Even though they step to the very edge of precipices and stop to nibble on flowers, riding up is a good option if you cannot walk.

Simple rules for riding up mountains on mules

- Lean forward on the uphill
- Lean backward on the downhill to help the mule balance
- Don't panic if the pony man drops the lead rope
- Let the animal to make its own way up the steeper slopes
- Let them eat the flowers. They're animals, flowers are food.

It's time to set out on the first walk, the hike up the Laxman Ganga, first to reach the confluence of the Laxman Ganga and the Bhyundar, and then to follow the Bhyundar valley up to Ghangaria.

CHAPTER 10

THE PATH TO GHANGARIA
SNOWS OF THE HIMALAYAS

> *Above all, do not lose your desire to walk: every day I*
> *walk myself into a state of well-being and walk away*
> *from every illness; I have walked myself into my best*
> *thoughts and I know of no thought so burdensome*
> *that one cannot walk away from it."*
>
> – *Søren Kierkegaard*

I t's crisp walking weather with a chance of masala chai as we shake out and fix the trekking poles, and with a last check of bootlaces, the long-awaited walk begins. With a laugh, and a cheer, we set out together, at least at the beginning, soon, we will separate as we walk at our own pace.

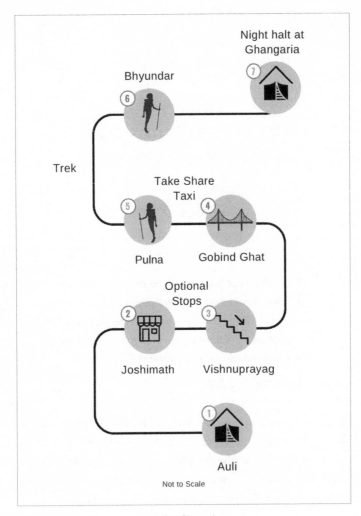

Auli to Ghangaria

Lush sub–tropical vegetation flourishes by the sides of the cobbled path and the river runs loud with high lacy waterfalls splashing down dark cliffs across the valley.

I take it slowly, as the air begins to thin, and tiredness can set in quicker than expected at these altitudes. Pavilions span the path with stone benches to sit down, take a rest, and enjoy the view, but it's too early in the walk. I pass by with a wave to fellow trekkers.

The path almost sparkles. Government sweepers keep the footpath clear of steaming mule droppings but armed with long brooms they also badger you relentlessly for tips.

I cross trekkers form all over India, and Sikh pilgrims, their hearts intent on Hemkund Sahib. It's not just us with an enormous thirst for adventure today, it's in our pilgrim heritage. Is that what drove us to this hard walk?

Glancing to the right, the Bhyundar Ganga flows swiftly, with little beaches and even the occasional terraced field, while across the valley, unnamed waterfalls tumble into the river from the steep gorge sides. Bursts of flowers bloom heedlessly by the sides of the path, Himalayan balsam peep out in flushes of pink. Tiny bees hover over golden daisies nestling under mossy grey-green rocks.

Higher, the air cools to form the occasional evanescent mist. I switch between sunhat and a warm hat and drop the poncho over my head as I adjust the trekking poles to cope with the sudden steepness of unevenly laid stones.

BHYUNDAR JUNCTION

A couple of hours of steady ascent, and Bhyundar village appears, a clutch of make-shift shops and scattered mud and stone dwellings on the hillsides. The Bhyundar Ganga joins the Laxman Ganga here to continue down to Gobind Ghat. Bhyundar is Pulna's summer grazing village where the shepherd families would drive their flocks to feed on the rich grasses of the high meadows, before moving them on to Tibet for sale.

The dilapidated huts scattered on the hillside reflect the vanishing nomadic lifestyle because of the closing of the mountain passes to Tibet. No longer do the lonely shepherds drive their shaggy herds of goat and sheep through the high passes beyond the lush meadows.

At the wide boulder–strewn confluence, we collapse in one of the myriad teahouses for a rest and lunch, happy to shrug off the day packs, and gulp down tea as we wait for piping hot *aloo parathas*.

I shudder at the fluorescent stacks of Maggi noodle packets, the blight of the Himalayan trails and indeed any tourist spot in India, from beach shacks in Goa to Himalayan teashops. The huge appetite for Maggi noodles gallops on unabated – and trekkers and tourists alike proclaim their love for this abomination. On the occasions when forced to eat Maggi noodles, I keep it a secret and atone for it by eating butter chicken or palak paneer at the first opportunity. Hot, cooked food, with minimal risk of food poisoning is what is needed not plastic encased junk.

While the steaming masala tea and water are better than all the soft drinks, there is no option for water except bottled water, but take care not to throw the bottle anywhere except in a bin. The Garhwal tourism department carries all the waste off the mountain, on mules.

THE CASE OF THE KILLER COW

At Bhyundar village, reality confronts us. The previous day, a fierce storm from the mountains funneled through the valley and tossed the iron bridge aside. Now only a fragile suspension bridge dangles over the raging boulder–rolling waters. No mules allowed on the bridge.

A rough path loops along a *nullah*, up a steep slope covered in deep vegetation, and we must inch up it to cross on a temporary bridge. Access to the bridge is via a rough path, on one side a deep stone lined channel, and on the other, the vertical wedge of hacked out earth towers above us. From higher up we hear the swish of grass cutting scythes, and the voice of village women. And then, out of the corner of my eye, something dark hurtles down towards my head. Instinctively I duck into the earth bank, pressing myself against the slope.

With a bellow, a black shadow slides over me–into our path– it's a backsliding cow. Tumbling backwards down the cutting, losing its footing and rolling over. Vibha goes flying over the edge–she grabs a branch of a young tree growing between the stones. She's hanging over the stone channel, held by the trembling branch. Rushing over I drag her up, and we lean panting against the side of the mountain, while a herd of more nimble–footed cows trot around the bend, followed by a wiry villager with a long stick, she's worried about the black cow, not near cow –killed trekkers.

The cow has clambered back on to all four legs and galloped off, terrifying more trekkers in its path. Vibha's only complaint was that I hadn't captured it on video, I gasp for air, relieved I'm not killed by a cow. I told you to beware of rampaging bovines.

We clamber uphill, past some desolate huts and take a sharp right turn downhill to the temporary suspension bridge, struggling over loose broken rocks, construction materials, coarse sand and pebbles. After the episode with the cow, I almost skip across the bridge. Anything to put some distance between us and killer cows. I almost miss it, at the far end of

SUSAN JAGANNATH

a side valley, are the lower slopes of the snow-covered massif of Hathi Parbat. Then we turn onto the track and it's lost to view.

After a short rest I tackle the last steep ascent to Ghangaria, our destination for the day. Towering conifers close in overhead, moss-covered boulders bloom with flowers below and above. Strings of mules decorated with bells, and gaily colored ribbons, plod up or down, carrying nervous riders clinging to the pommels with sweaty palms. Strings of mules with tightly lashed crates of food or lumpy construction material struggle up the broken stone path. And beside them the sure-footed pony boys or men run alongside, shouting encouragement or abuse at the mules at every "last turn". I catch up with Vibha here and we want to walk in together, nearly there goes on for some time.

GLAMPING AT THE HELIPAD

The forest ends abruptly, and we emerge onto a wide flat meadow and in front, Rataban glows though the cleft of the steep valley. Myriad delicate waterfalls tumble down from remnants of glaciers clinging to the sides of the gorge.

I stop, leaning on the trekking poles to gaze at a swaying encampment of tents. Rows and rows of "Swiss tents", with rooms and vestibules to sit out are the luxury accommodation, and booked up to a year earlier. Looking out, there are vistas of the mountain, meadow and glacier, and all day, the buzzing sound of helicopters landing and taking off from the helipad.

Gripping the trekking poles and shaking out my legs get moving again we pass the glamour of the tent city, up the path that disappears into the last grove of Himalayan pines.

Something jingles ahead, and there's a flat area where a herd of mules fidget and toss their heads to flick flies from their eyes.

INTO GHANGARIA

Other trekkers stop off at the GMVN tourist cabins and huts that dominate the entrance set among patches of lawn with bricked over paths. Moving on backpacker hostel–like accommodation and to "luxury" hotels alike are identified by temporary polyester banners, there's an impermanence here, like all of Ghangaria.

We peer through glass–paned polished wooden windows at eating areas laid out neatly with tables and chairs. Reading the menus, it looks like they serve mostly Punjabi food, or generic Indian food, sweets and tea. On the roadside stalls, the smell of hot Samosas and pakoras being fried in huge pans tempt us to stop. The best thing you can get after a day's walk is the hot pakoras and or jelabis, to go with your steel tumblers of tea. But ahead we see something more tempting, a room set up with chairs and foot massagers, excellent after a day of walking, and we stop to get the most reviving foot massage ever.

At last, we're here. Fast walkers Shanti and Anju cheer us on from the upper floors. Oops, some more climbing, but I'm elated, looking at my Fitbit. We've walked into Ghangaria about 4 hours after leaving Pulna. Utterly exhausted I collapse onto one of the three beds and waiting for hot water to come up for our ablutions, I snooze lightly before reviving hot tea, pakoras and jelabis come up to us. Sitting on the verandah outside, we consider the narrow street below, and the towering walls of a mountain, while we sip the tea and enjoy another foot massage from a masseur. Tiredness vanishes.

We set out to explore the one–street town, one gurudwara, one guru–ka–langar, and lots of hotels and shops with walking gear for hire. We peer through the grubby glass panes of a shut bookshop, and realize, it's already time for dinner.

Darkness falls. We walk down to Gangotri, where the first dinner is hot *aloo kulcha* and *chole,* or stuffed bread and chickpea curry. This is delicious, spicy and piping hot straight from the tandoor. The restaurant is abuzz with a happy crowd of trekkers from all over India and the world, and the waiter flies between the tables, heaping up the plates with hot rotis and kulchas, refilling the bowls with channa, and offering us more tea and hot gulab jamuns swimming in a saffron scented syrup.

Eat well, I tell myself, knowing that by tomorrow, at these altitudes, my appetite will drop off.

We are here. Tomorrow is the day we walk up to the target, the Valley of Flowers. I clamber into my sleep sack and drag the thick coverlets and colorful blankets over me. I hope for the sweet embrace of sleep. The Diamox is working, and unlike earlier high–altitude treks, I fall asleep.

CHAPTER 11
FRAGRANCE AND FIRE
POIGNANT AND SUBTLE AND BITTER PERFUME

*P*OIGNANT *and subtle and bitter perfume,*

Exquisite, luminous, passionate bloom,

Your leaves interwoven of fragrance and fire

Are Savitri's sorrow and Sita's desire,

Draupadi's longing, Damayanti's fears,

And sweetest Sakuntala's magical tears.

—*Sarojini Naidu*

Day Five dawns cool and misty, I throw off the covers to rush to the window and gaze at the looming mountain, the silent snow topped massif does nothing to deter me – today our destination is in sight. But first the sharp rap at the door, the hotel boy has carried up buckets of hot water for wood-scented bathing.

Mugs of warm water splash over chilled limbs banish the last vestiges of sleep. Refreshed and ready I look down at the clattering lane bustling with porters, ponies and people. I don't quite know what lies ahead. Given how busy Ghangaria is early in the morning, I dread a crowded track.

FOOTSTEPS OF TIME

I snap up my umbrella and slip down through misty drizzle to the restaurant, bright and bustling with hearty breakfasts for all. The waiter urges us to eat more, the climb ahead is strenuous and long, he warns. Picking up our packed lunch and water, we pass the shops that line the narrow lanes with everything you could possibly need, from warm hats, cheap ponchos, socks and shoes, to hot samosas and cold jelabis. A tip, the curly saffron sweet are tossed out of bubbling oil later in the day, so if you must eat *jelabis* for breakfast, be aware that they are yesterday's fare.

Blue tarp roofs flap over wide enclosures of mules and muleteers, and where there are mules there is the earthy horsey smell of dung. But soon it will be only the fragrance of flowers, as no mules are allowed in the Valley of Flowers.

Ghangaria unfolds as a grubby shanty town, narrow streets make sharp jagged turns − there are little to no views except the sides of the gorge. It's a rainy monsoon day the sides of the mountain appear dank and threatening. I quicken my step, past the cobbled streets, the laden mules with decorated faces and flicking tails, and out onto bridge, facing a triple waterfall and melting glacier.

I breathe deep of the already thinning air, I need every ounce of air on the steep ascent to the Valley of Flowers. I'm prepared for altitude sickness and exhaustion and brain freeze. I've taken my daily Diamox, better a little toe tingling, than Acute Mountain Sickness (AMS) or worse, HAPE (high altitude pulmonary edema).[1]

CHOOSING DANGEROUS PATHS

It's 7 a.m., the earliest time we're allowed in, so I calculate to reach the upper valley by 10:30 a.m., or 11:00 a.m. Others hire a porter with a precarious pittoo basket and prepare to be carried aloft. I try out a *pittoo* for a few steps watching for swipes from lowering silver birches, and fear of sudden slips that can tumble basket and human contents into the raging river far below. There are no statistics of how many people die this way, and I suspect that my fears are unfounded. But, thank you, I descend, relieved to be alive and on my own two feet.

I cross the bridge over a melting glacier, where the Laxman Ganga sparkles coyly out of its arched cavern. Above, it thunders down from the mountainside in three levels of waterfalls, from gorge walls so high that you can barely see the top however far back you crane your neck. To the left is the rocky confluence where the Pushpavati meets the Laxman Ganga and continues down to join the Alaknanda as the Bhyundar Ganga.

The boulder strewn bed gleams with silver streams, and away from the torrent, tiny birds flit from rock to rock. It's a gleaming rockscape of plunging gorges, glaciers and glittering raindrops. It seems impossible that somewhere higher than all this could even exist.

In Indian mythology, the Pandavas named the Pushpavati river so when they saw the myriad *Pushpa* or flowers floating downstream as they toiled their way up the mountains in search of redemption. Maybe, at other times of the year, the

Pushpavati is a calmer stream, but not in the monsoon. Is this even the same river? Who knows, myth and magic intermingle, and I give up puzzling over it.

The image of the Valley of Flowers as a peaceful bower is replaced by the reality of thunderous black gorges and steep paths. The rain buckets down and I pull up the hood of my unglamorous hooded poncho. Wet hands grip the poles as the path climbs to a steaming, tin-covered booth where I push through the clamour, to pay for my pass, a grubby little piece of paper, or *chitti*, for this shard of paradise.

Chitti is an Indian word has entered the English language as "chit", a piece of paper that is a record that you have paid for some privilege. It is just one of the thousands of Indian words that turned into bonafide English words thanks to the 200-year-old interaction between India and the East India Company.[2]

The pass allows me entry for three consecutive days, but I must exit the valley by 5 pm every day, a narrow window to climb up and wander about looking for flowers. The raised booth is packed with porters and baskets, guides and trekkers, I grab my chit and escape down a narrow path with green and orange railings. The vegetation changes, and more conifers soar

above the sub-tropical plants. Here is the first of the arum lilies, or cobra lilies, a rather threatening-looking plant that looks like a cobra ready to strike.

THE FAIRY GATE

Further on, is a cave tucked into the side of the gorge, and painted on the rock are the words, "Blue Poppy", alerting us to the only place where blue poppies grow. The cup-shaped blue flower, is not a real poppy, its shape and delicate crepe – like petals make it look like a poppy.[3] Where does the rare sky–blue color come from? It comes from the pigment delphinidin that combines with the plant's ability to grow in the acidic soils of Himalayan rock slopes. If you were to try to grow blue poppies at home in an alkaline soil, the color would be more violet than the clear sky–blue of Mecopnosis, the correct name.

The black, plunging rock walls of an immense dark gorge surround us, overhead grey clouds shroud the sky from view and beneath our boots, pounds the rock–tumbling torrent of the Pushpavati, or Byundar river. The correct name eludes me, as one insouciant villager shrugged,

These myriad rivers and waterfalls have no name, they appear and disappear.

As we do.

Frank Smythe called the entire valley the Bhyundar valley, and the stream as the Byundar river, but others claim it is the Pushpavati, mentioned in the Mahabharata, the flower–filled stream that the Pandavas walked along on their ascent to Heaven.

I prefer the name Bhyundar, the fearful torrent.

A recent rockslide has tossed craggy boulders across the path, contemptuous of the flimsy balusters. Guides and porters glance mountainwards, hustling us over the rockslide towards a rickety bridge dangling dangerously over the torrent. A graphic sign depicts the next two kilometers as a wiggly line. Heed the ill drawn sketch. Truth comes in strange disguises.

This twisting, rocky riverbed, racked with rubble and moraine, and slashed with ruthless rockslides is incongruously named "Dwari Pairi", the Fairy Gate. The local mountain people considered it the door to the realm of fairies. Perhaps there was no other way these massive boulders could be tossed midstream forming impromptu waterfalls. I doubt these powerful Himalayan fairies are related to the delicate beings in children's books.

I breathe in, adjust my poncho and steady my legs before I step onto the flimsy bridge that shudders with the power of the river. I cross it, and start the steep ascent, scrambling over the broken rocks, using the trekking poles to balance. The rain pelts down harder, and we hurry to leave the furious funnel of "Fairy Gate".

THE REALITY OF THE TREK

A series of sharp switchbacks lifts us away from the valley floor and up to the misty skies. It's a risk, will I reach the valley today or will the steep climb and the oncoming rain defeat you? I decrease the height of my trekking poles and then adjust my grip, before climbing. On this route, they are vital. The air thins, and I slow down.

Porters with *pittoos* and people on their backs pass me, the people swathed in plastic to keep them dry. It must be stifling in there, in mind and body. Wrapped like so much baggage in the porter's baskets, the non-walkers peer out anxiously, holding still as the porter takes one tentative step after the other on the wet and jagged path. The weight gets heavier and heavier as the porter tires, and the air thins. One slip and the basket can plunge down to the river, tumbling over and over to smash onto the rocks below.

Pre–2013, this path was a steady three kilometer walk to the valley of flowers at a gentle incline. Today it is a five kilometer hack up the sides of the gorge and over the headland. One kilometer of it is a vertiginous ascent to reach the ridge.

I'm careful of slips and trips on the path cobbled with sharp-edged embedded rocks. You might expect a "cobbled" path to comprise flattened stones, here the cobbles are embedded with the ankle-twisting narrow edges facing upwards. This makes it more difficult for the mountain to shrug the path off and fling it into the river. Yet through these harsh grey rocks a delicate flower pushes out its tiny fragile head. I step over it so as not to crush the perfect white bloom.

Higher, the rain slows and there are the cloud wreathed walls of the gorge on one side and resin scented conifers on the other. Pine, oak and white-trunked silver birches blanket the steep slopes. The dappled white and grey trunks of the silver birches remind me of home, and the silver gums of Australia. Their papery white and black bark are so apt for a writer's imagination. In fact, legend says, the bark was used to write on, much like paper. I rest on a low wall protecting the path, waiting for Vibha. Shanti and Anju have long vanished up the path.

The climb seems endless, switchback after switchback, with occasional glimpses either of the vertiginous sheer rockfaces of the gorge, or the threadlike path on the opposite side. That is the path to Hemkund Sahib. The blue tarp covered teashops on the way are like tiny toys, even smaller than a Lego block.

LONGING

Walking with the mountains underfoot and overhead and all around; the cold, the climb and the crowds swallow me whole into the heart of the Himalayas. Tumbled rocks and sharp switchbacks interrupt the cadence of the climb, forcing me to squeeze against the rocky walls to give way to the downhill traffic. On the first day it's like the conga line to Everest, will I find the Valley of Flowers trampled to death by unruly mobs?

White–barked silver birches lean over the path, brushing the hiker's heads, and on either side the flowers and plants crowd the path, shrinking it to a bare thread of cobbles. Climbing higher, light trickles through the thinning conifers and an entire side of the valley flushes pink with waving banks of Himalayan balsam.

The path opens up as the top of the ridge appears, and the stony track transforms to the gently sloping path promised by other guidebooks. The rain continues, no valley vistas yet. We stop for a rest in a cave with a dry sandy floor, tucked into a craggy outcrop. I lean against the cold rocky wall. I try not to sit down at all while walking, as it becomes harder to start again, the walking rhythm broken.

In the distance through the misty rain, a line of walkers in dark hoods shuffle along, are these a queue of hobbits, and if so, where is Gandalf?[4]

I do find Gandalf on another day – but that is another story. For now, it is one step after another in my well worn in boots and thick socks. I've lost sight of Shanti in the line ahead or behind, I hope those repaired boots of hers are holding up.

Ahead around any of these curves is the Valley of Flowers.

CHAPTER 12

EXCELSIS

VISTAS OF ALP, FOREST, SNOW-FIELD AND PEAK

> *Is there any region of the Himalayas, or even of the world, to excel this region in beauty and grandeur? Where else are there to be found such narrow and precipitous valleys and gorges, such serene vistas of alp, forest, snow-field and peak?*

— *Frank Smythe*

Up a series of stepped landings and around a curve, the first sparkling glacier stream twinkles out in joyful greeting. The glacier has retreated, and the ice–blue brook flows out from underneath the frozen arches to babble over the rocks and moss. We creak across the rough–hewn bridge and I sink down to the stream cupping the icy water in my hand to sip and then splash on my face. Holy water! Closing my eyes, I breathe in the scent of ice and blooms, and listen to the "Ommm" of humming bees.

DARSHAN

It's not a coincidence that this feels like worship. Ten thousand years of awe or *darshan* of these mountains well up in me. A lingering legacy from ancestors who gazed at these mountains and wove them into a lasting mythology. Darshan is a two-way action, you look at God and He looks back at you. No words needed. From me "I am here, Lord", and in reply, a simple all-encompassing "I am".

Above me lush green meadows soften the harsh edges of the peaks, and the entire valley lies ahead. The sun comes out on a verdant flower-speckled space ringed by snowy peaks that look close enough to touch. As we are so high, the peaks are no longer leering overhead instead they are a picture-perfect range of snowy peaks like the cupped hand of God. "I will hold you in the palm of my Hand."

BAMAN DAUR OR THE BOULDER GATE

Perching on a dryish riverside boulder, I rummage through my backpack, before I unlace boots and peel off socks. Wiggling my toes and rotating my ankles is so relaxing that I'm tempted to plunge my feet in the water, but no, others are drinking from it downstream.

Clean socks are my secret weapon in the war against walking weariness. And on this trip instead of my usual three pairs of socks, I have carried eight pairs. One of those clean dry pairs goes on, and the used socks crumple into a pocket in my backpack. I lace my boots up firmly with fingers half frozen from the glacial stream, as my toes tingle with tiredness, and Diamox.

After the stream the towering boulder marks the visual start of the valley. It's where everyone sits down for a picnic lunch. A group sit down and begin handing round hot drinks, cold drinks and food, with laughter and a lot of clutter they eat and make merry.

I leave.

We will eat on our way down, time is too precious to waste on picnicking. Not that I don't enjoy picnicking, thanks to my adventurous parents, I've picnicked from Kashmir to Kanyakumari, and Amritsar to Arunachal Pradesh, but given the narrow sliver of time in this valley, I'd rather be walking. Alone or with my friends, in this space, I am not inclined to talk to strangers.

IN THE FOOTSTEPS OF FATE

Pushing onwards or skywards might be more appropriate, the grim gorges and rough rockslides are replaced by meadows lush with a green never seen on the plains, and embankments of flowers, through it all the sound of running water. We are now treading in the footsteps of the early explorers like Frank Smythe and Joan Legge. [1]

Frank Smythe, an early twentieth-century mountaineer, discovered the valley and then returned here to camp for months recording and gathering plants. Was he a mountaineer or a technical writer? What a glorious way to produce a manual! Or a travel book.

In a classic real-life twist of six degrees of separation, only two degrees separate Frank Smythe from myself. In a spot of research, I find that he contracted malaria in Darjeeling, and later died of it. And he was in Darjeeling to plan another expedition with Tenzing Norgay, and as every one who lived in Darjeeling knows, you would always bump into Mr. Tenzing Norgay, either at a school or college talk, in the Himalayan Mountaineering Institute, or on the Mall or Chaurasta in "Darj".

It is appropriate that Frank Smythe is remembered with fondness and admiration in both Hindi and English, at the ECO center in Ghangaria, where you can watch a short documentary about the Valley of Flowers, and his journey.

Frank Smythe is forgotten today, except in the Valley of Flowers, or bookshops in Uttarakhand where you can pick up his famous book, The Valley of Flowers.[2]

CHAPTER 13
DEATH IN THE MEADOW
LONGING

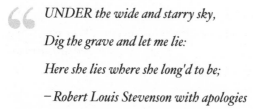

> *UNDER the wide and starry sky,*
>
> *Dig the grave and let me lie:*
>
> *Here she lies where she long'd to be;*
>
> *– Robert Louis Stevenson with apologies*

The rain lifts and in the brilliant mountain sunshine, the raindrops sparkle on the flowers. Tiny drops of flower rain shower us as we forge through lush paths strewn with fresh–fallen blossoms. Every week different varieties of flowers burst out in an urgent rush from seed to bloom to seed. In early August it is the pink of Himalayan balsam that predominates, interspersed with towering banks of milk parsley, waving their lacy spheres across meadows and up rocky crags. Mixed in with pink spires of Himalayan knotweed and balsam are the perfect purple blooms of geranium wallichinum.

We push on in the thin air and jump the streams to where the meadows and tiny valleys seem to wander up and get lost in the sky. Remnants of glaciers glitter in the sun, pearly white from a distance, they hang like jeweled necklaces on the up-rushing black crags. Nestled in the tiny valleys and encrusted with moraine and a load of rubble, the glacier's not so pretty.

We hustle along, no time to eat here, as time in the Valley is precious. We arrived here at noon, (the gate only opens at 7 a.m.), and we must be out before 5:00 p.m. or earlier if the clouds close in. Our guide hustles us to leave by 2:00 p.m. Don't be deceived by the thought that walking downhill will be quicker. It is not. The steep slope and frequent mists mean that you must watch every step. And there is no phone coverage in the valley, so if you get in trouble, you may be alone.

Today this is not a problem, there are plenty of people wandering about, and as we leave, we meet walkers sauntering in. I wonder how much they will see, as you need at least two hours inside the valley, past the boulder gate.

AN ADVENTUROUS WOMAN

In the midst of this most Hindu of valleys, lies a lonely grave with a carved cross and the words of Psalm 121.

"I will lift up mine eyes unto the hills, from whence cometh my help." [1]

We arrive at the grave of Joan Margaret Legge, botanist, adventurer, aristocrat. She trekked here alone, to document the plants of the valley. Unfortunately, she lived too danger-ously and within a week of setting up camp, slipped and fell to her death.

Her grave lies by the stream in sight of the mountains. A bit of research reveals that she was Lady Joan Margaret, the daughter of an Earl, hence able to travel and adventure on her own. A brave woman, to trek here alone at 54. If there was an adventurer who gave her all, here she is where she lies at rest in the heart of the Himalayas.

THE THREE ZONES

For the average hiker and tourist there are three zones that you can access safely, without meeting the fate of Joan Margaret Legge.

The first zone is when you cross the first stream and arrive at the large boulder, called Baman Daur. Walk on further and you come to an intersection.

The second zone is the meadow where the flowers, and streams surround the grave, and in the distance the tall green conifers wave gently in the breezes.

The third zone is the higher saucer shaped zone ascending to the cloud wrapped peaks.

RIVER BEAUTY ON THE BANKS OF THE PUSHPAVATI

We follow the paths leading over the moraine and birch forest to the riverbed of the Pushpavati, this is about 3 kilometers from the Baman Daur. All along the banks are clusters of pink River beauty, blue kashmirayana and creeping snowberry, with its bright blue berries that taste and smell like the old faithful, Vicks Vaporub.

We must have walked about seven of the ten kilometers length, only looking up to the end where it passes the foot of Rataban, beyond which is the Byundar pass. This area is unique because it is the transition zone between the Greater

Himalaya and the Zanskar ranges, beyond are the dry hills of Tibet, truly at the edge of the roof of the world.

To see more of it, we use two of the three–day passes to the fullest, and hike in every day, trying to walk as far as possible into the valley even to the very end.

On the second day, a local guide from the Valley of Flowers interpretation center in Ghangaria joined our party. Thanks to her we could walk to the bed of the Pushpavati and beyond, crossing bubbling brooks and past sparkling fields of edelweiss, pink river beauty and clusters of blue Kashmir corydalis.

By walking further, we saw different views and vegetations, more streams, melting glaciers and past lush meadows full of fine grass interspersed with banks of yellow sunflower like showy inula, and stands of Cortia wallichaina or Himalayan silge.

The second day that we visited, the valley was nearly empty of people, and as we went deeper in the valley, it was as if we were alone in the world of enchantment.

COMING DOWN

Every afternoon we descended, taking infinite care on the two–hour trail down. The descent to the gorge and the metal bridge at Dwari Pairi gorge is steep, slippery and twisting. In the twilight missteps are easy, and a mistake can cost you a broken limb, or even death. As we tread out of the valley, the rain tumbles down and we seek shelter in the cave near the valley entrance above the tree line. It's crowded with others, and we remember to pull out our packed lunches. I pack the wrappings to take down the mountain with us.

Monsoonal rain rolls in, the clouds swirl up from the steamy plains and as they reach the soaring barrier of the Himalayas; they drop their load of moisture and continue over the dry plains of Tibet. The kiss of rain and the intermittent winds blow us downwards.

I shrug on the poncho, and adjust the trekking poles for downhill walking, as I set off for Ghangaria for the last time through pine, silver birch and flowers peeping out at every step. A lengthy walk, almost as tiring as we watch every step. A couple of brash teens slither between switch backs, pummeling into mud and bushes. We plunge down deeper into the gorge, and the sun vanishes as an early twilight creeps along the valley floor, as the sun begins to slip behind the towering mountains. Round the last curving switchback and we arrive back at the black maw of Dwairi Pari.

We climb back to the valley that opens up again before us with Ghangaria steaming gently in the distance. The National Park booth is clamorous with exiting hikers and porters, and we join in shouting out our names and are marked out and waved through. The park closes at 5 pm, and the rangers wait to tick us off the list as we exit.

Back in Ghangaria, we kick off boots and hang the rain gear out to dry. Masala tea, hot pakoras and jelabis sustain us until dinner time. I sit on the verandah, and close my eyes, the sights of the Valley still float before my closed eyes. It is only 6:00 p.m., and it is already dusk. I contemplate going straight to bed, but a long dinner with conversation with friends in the quiet restaurant is a satisfying end to busy days.

CHAPTER 14
PILGRIMS PROGRESS
DEVOTION

> *I seek a place that can never be destroyed, one that is pure, and that fadeth not away, and it is laid up in heaven, and safe there, to be given, at the time appointed, to them that seek it with all their heart*
>
> — *John Bunyan, The Pilgrim's Progress*

The alchemy of the Valley of Flowers is that you can switch between tourist, hiker and pilgrim in a day, or you can be all three. After our valley explorations, it was time to climb to Hemkund Tal, the glittering glacial lake that boasts the highest gurdwara in the world.

It is also the site of a mythic dream sequence. Hemkund is the place that the tenth guru, Guru Gobind Singh saw in a dream. From the burning plains of the Punjab he had a vision of meditating here in a past life. It was this meditation in the lap of the gods that gave him the strength and courage to continue his mission on earth, creating a religion for all to serve one God.

Jo Bole so Nihal and *Sat Sri Akaal* is the cry and response that we hear all the winding way up to Hemkund Sahib, the star-shaped Sikh temple that looks like a Swiss chalet nestling beneath soaring peaks and reflected in the crystal clear waters of the tarn. Some say it's the shape of an inverted lotus. The five entrances are to allow pilgrims to enter from every direction.

The site is sacred to the tenth Guru, Gobind Singh. Guru Gobind, his father and four sons were all brutally executed, or fell in battle for refusing to convert to Islam, in the 16th century.

A large Sikh family from the *pind* trudge down, greeting me as I check the way for the next day's walk. Villagers, with work clothes, slippers and a tired joyful glow, they smile as they head for the Gurudwara; plastic rice sacks covering their heads from the evening rain.

MATHA-JEE

The morning dawns clear, but during breakfast (more *aloo parathas*) the torrent begins, and we decide to wait out the heaviest downpour. An hour later it's time to go, rain or not. Draped in our ponchos, we set out on the road to Hemkund in a steady drizzle, past the Gurudwara that has already emptied of pilgrims, past the temporary blue-tarped mule sheds and onto the bridge, where a triple waterfall falls to the last lingering remnants of the Laxman Ganga glacier.

All along the narrow stone path, pilgrims mount up uncertainly on fidgety mules, clutching the pommels of the saddles with a death grip. The 6-kilometer 6-hour path up to the lake slashes switchback after switchback all the way up the steep valley of the Laxman Ganga, and while it is paved all the way, at many spots the fragile–looking railings have collapsed, and the stone flags wobble and slip underfoot enough for me to trip and fall. No lasting damage, more embarrassment as pilgrims rush to help me up with cries of "*Matha–jee. Aap theek ho?*". Did I fall over an old woman? Then I realize the term is addressed to me by worried pilgrims.

"Yes, theek hu", I assure them.

That's almost "Reverend Mother" – a sign that I'm now well past the age of being leered at or harassed in India.

I dust myself off, assure them I'm ok, and sit a while to catch my breath, and flex my legs and arms to ensure there's no damage. And muse on my "Reverend Mother" status. A smile escapes, how the exasperated nuns of my convent years would have chuckled at this!

I am lost in a crowd that sweeps around the corner. Grand-mothers helped up by grandsons, tiny drooly babies clasped tenderly by their tough pink–turbaned Dads, beautiful women with perfect makeup and exquisitely coiled hair, toil up the steep and slippery stony path with shouts of *Sat Sri Akal* or The One Lord is True. Their passion interleaves with pain and sheer glamour. I feel under–dressed in my hike clothes and serviceable grey poncho. I pull out my red scarf and drape it round my throat for a flash of color. Next time, I may even pack my makeup kit!

Pilgrims converge from all over India, and the world – including Afghanistan – a reminder that the Sikhs once ruled from Afghanistan to Lahore and beyond reclaiming all the land (and the Kohinoor) taken by Nadir Shah in his rapacious conquest of Mughal treasure.

The gurudwara nestles beside another kind of gem, an icy lake near the top of the Himalayas.

ASCENDING TO HEAVEN

Ghangaria recedes to an insignificant speck, and Himalayan oak and broad–leaved rhododendron overhang the path. Beneath them where patches of sunlight light up the ground, masses of golden daisies, blue corydalis and pink impatiens peep out at us. Today as we toil upwards, the path takes us above the tree line; the peaks surround us, glaciers confront us and the path is often clouded over by fine mist, or rain. And pink bistorta, potentilla and forget–me–nots splash the sheer rocky ledges with glowing colors.

In a while the rain recedes, or we walk above it, but it is not worth removing our rain gear. This walk is a brutal slog, I can't decide whether it is harder than that of the valley of flowers. That was one kilometer of steep ascent, this is all 6 kilometers of switchback, the stone flags alternate with rubble, and once past the tree line we stop at a clutch of tea houses, reviving hot sweet tea is needed.

We are at 4000 meters here, and the Diamox is working. I have no feelings of AMS, except perhaps a lack of appetite. In contrast at this altitude at Sandakphu, I was sick and giddy. A recent study reveals that Acute Mountain Sickness affects a third of the pilgrims walking up to Hemkund Sahib, mostly brought about by an ignorance of the condition. With 150,000 pilgrims a year, that is 50,000 persons. Fortunately, no one can stay here longer than a few hours, so descent to Ghangaria solves the problem of altitude sickness.

A young woman weeps with every staggering step, her mascara smudging down her cheeks, overcome with a headache and nausea. Getting her to sit down I give her cough lozenges, and aspirin for her headache. I sit by her, my arm around her heaving shoulders till her sobs subside to a breathy moan.

She's crying for something else too, she hasn't seen her babies for a year, if she doesn't make it to the gurudwara, she sobs, she may never see them again. She asks me to pray for her children, I assure her that I will, and she wipes her tears and smudged mascara off with a tissue that I hand her and hugs me back. Maybe she needs her mother here.

So many people cross our paths, pilgrims all, in this interlude in our busy lives. From solemn–eyed women to riotous groups of bikers up from Ludhiana, in bright pink turbans. Pink is the color of pilgrimage today in Hemkund. If brawny, bristly bearded Sikh men want to wear pink, I'm not about to object.

CROSSING THE GLACIER

Far above the tree–line, the road pierces a retreating glacier that slumps across the slope like a sleeping dragon with a dripping nose. A wall of ice towers over posturing pilgrims, and we must wait for our turn to cross. Icy water oozes across the road, making this a damp crossing. In June, when the path first opens every year, pilgrims must trudge up the drip-ping path between steep buttresses of ice for the final two kilometers.

Propping my trekking poles against a boulder, I place my foot on it and tighten the laces of my thick–soled boots. My head swims even with this slight bending, and I lift my head care-fully and wait for the dizziness to subside.

On one side, the glacier, on the other the meltwater drips over the side of the road coalescing into a pounding stream that waterfalls off a cliff further down the steep slope. The meltwater gurgles over two levels of heaped rocks and disappears with a roar down the mountainside in a hurry to reach the plains, in contrast to the creeping pilgrims struggling upwards towards the heavens.

Ghangaria fades into nothingness as a lacy mist swirls down from the peaks, and ghost–like a cloud rises up from the valleys below. The sides of the gorge steepen, and, "garden" beds of flowers bloom on every rocky shelf. Including the elusive blue poppy in clumps that nod and bow their sky–blue cups in the chilly breezes. I wonder at the how wild winds don't shred the delicate petals. Today though, the wind has dropped, and the rain has slowed to a light drizzle. In patches, puce candle blooms appear, rosy Himalayan fleece and fluffy coral pink bistorta, standing tall in clumps in all the world as it planted here by a gardener with an eye for ethereal beauty. Purple flowers flutter, these are gentians, not poppies, but the purple, blue and pink are ideal for any little girl crazy for rainbow unicorns.

Stolid mules with bells and plaited tails fill in for prancing unicorns. A muleteer appropriates the camera phone of a rider and clambers up the steep slope to click photos of the flowers, and the rider.

THE BRAHMAKAMAL

As we round another cliff, there are the unmistakable clumps of the pride of Garhwal, the Brahmakamal, a huge lotus that blooms once every 12 years at these altitudes of rarefied air, waiting for the perfect conjunction of well–drained rock, a patch of soil and just enough sun to unfold its huge petals to the radiant rays of a Himalayan summer sun.

The Brahmakamal is so precious and endangered that the villagers of Pulna, pluck only one flower a year, for their festival. No one else is allowed to take these delicate blooms of a pale goldy-green in a perfect whorl of softness nestling in a cape of dark green leaves. The closed buds are about to bloom, and in the shelter of the dripping rocks glow almost phosphorescent against the dark rocks of steep slopes.

Beyond, resolute clumps of bushes cling to the cliffs, with yellow flowers at the tips, rare Himalayan ginseng or rhodiola. The ginseng increases circulation and uptake of oxygen, exactly what you need in these climbs, where less oxygen can thicken the blood.

Ahead a long flight of grey stairs disappears into the sky. This is a "shortcut" of 1200 steps. With no more mountain above the stair – I must be at the top or nearly there, but I keep on the twisting path, and avoid the slippery steps.

On Himalayan treks, the end tantalizes you long before you arrive at your destination, and the curling smoke of teashops and the flapping blue of temporary tarps draw us on with their false imminence. Time stretches inexorably on upward slopes, leaping ahead in long strides.

On the way down, this is where I meet despairing pilgrims, asking how far to the top, and I always reply with – just a little way – Sat Sri Akal. A little white lie when time and distance have no meaning here at the top of the world.

HEMKUND SAHIB

With one last pull and push on my trekking poles, the last switchback is negotiated and ducking down beneath the blue tarps, I enter a narrow path lined with shops selling goods and shawls to offer at the shrine. Gleaming silken shawls in pink, orange and purple jostle hard steel bangles, and other offerings.

To the left a darkened flight of stairs lead down to bank of grim–looking toilets. I push open the door to the "Ladies", and blink in the darkness, the solar lights must be off, for there is no light except a dim glow from narrow slits set high in the damp wall. Thank goodness for phone flashlights but oh for my headlamp forgotten back in the room in Ghangaria.

Up the stairs and one last right turn, and the sacred destination is mirrored in the emerald waters of the lake. The lake reflects the green slopes, rocks and the clouds, and only a splatter of raindrops interrupts the perfect image in the water. A circular group of peaks crowd around the lake, and down from them creep thin threads of glaciers.

The seats in the shed are welcoming and dry, and I join the rest of the pilgrims shucking off shoes. I lean back, the weight off my feet, and I take a large breath of the thin pure air before tiptoeing into the lake. Wait.

There is a guy who goes on and on – shoes off, socks off, shirt off, hiking pants off...stop please. Cheered on by his friends, he tiptoes in looking for a flat spot in the rocky floor of the lake, he wades out slowly into the freezing water, before a sudden plunge, a faster leap up, and a splashing rush to the shore. His friends laugh and chuck a towel at his shivering shoulders.

I lift a doubtful foot. I'm not proving any points here. I dip an uncertain toe into the frigid waters and beat a quick retreat. The only ablution today will be back in the hotel – that wood–scented hot water in the bucket seems a treat.

Some water is to be looked at, and some to be bathed in, and ne'er the twain shall meet.

A forlorn Laxman temple nestles up to the gurudwara, one of the only shrines dedicated to Laxman alone. It is locked up, a concrete box enclosing a dark alcove with a barely visible idol.

In the open shining halls of the gurudwara, the Guru Granth Sahib is being chanted. I like Sikhism, the object of their veneration in the temple is a book – the ultimate Guru.

THE LAKE AND THE SPEAR

Hemkund, the name derives from the words Hem ("Snow") and Kund ("bowl"). The tarn is surrounded by seven snow-wreathed peaks. and since you are at 4600 meters, they don't seem too much higher than you. This is a lake dangling in the sky, held up by threads of waning glaciers and cupped by a bowl of slotted shale.

I half hope that a Sikh King Arthur Singh will appear on a rearing horse and toss a gleaming Excalibur into the still waters, with the Lady of the Lake seizing it and disappearing into the depths of Hemkund Sahib with scarcely a ripple.

In a surreal time shift, a Sikh priest in flowing saffron robes and a towering turban strides barefoot out of the temple, his medieval magnificence completed with a shining spear flut-tering with tassels of gold. Behind him, the chants from the Gurudwara fade into silence. The spear is ceremonial only, there will be no impaling of heretics today. Neither will he toss it into the lake. His stern face relents as I ask for a photo with him.

There was no way to do a *parikrama* round the lake. Stern warnings prohibit this is in multiple languages, so we line up at gurudwara, place our shoes carefully in a row of lockers and enter the temple barefoot and with our heads covered.

A MARTIAL TOUCH

You can tell that the gurudwara was built by army engineers where strength is the key. It is more of a bunker than a cathedral, an apt reflection of the Sikh's military tradition. Built of stark concrete blocks, massive steel beams hold up the multi-alcove steep sloped roof to betray a tale of a brutal winter. Nothing about the gurudwara detracts from the soaring amphitheater that nature provides, with steep rock walls above and a limpid lake glimmering beneath.

Open for a scant four months of the year, snow and ice attempt to grind it into the lake for the long and biting winter. The remorseless glacier sees everyone off the mountains by early October, with the path opening only in June after a hard scrabble by volunteers and the army from mid May. I snatch a brief moment in the carpet–lined hall before the covered altar. A rich fabric canopy hangs over it, and it's surrounded by gilt railings and plastic flowers. A handful of pilgrims sit in the hall, under the rafters draped with garlands and flowers.

Outside, the gentle persistent patter of rain forms a chorus with the sighing of quiet winds. I know that this can change in a moment, as afternoon approaches, the warm air rising from the plains far below collides with the cold air of the high Himalayas, causing, the monsoon,

After a six kilometer walk and a climb of over 1000 meters – we need food. We join the queue to the *guru ka langar* for just a few minutes. Unlike other langars, there is no sitting on the floor here, but on benches that line the langar. After a simple meal of delicious *khichdi* (rice and dal) washed down with hot sweet tea, it's time to go, as no one can stay beyond 2 p.m.

THE POWER OF A VOW

The clouds and threatening rain make the steep path slippery and dangerous. But I prefer to walk, despite the importuning of many muleteers. I do not understand how mules judge edges and heights, but I'm unwilling to risk my neck and life to the broken toenail of a recalcitrant mule. The mules are mostly well fed and well looked after, caparisoned with colorful braids and ribbons. There's always a lead mule, who decides the stop and start times of the meandering way. While mules are not allowed in the Valley of Flowers, they are allowed here, a boon for the many older pilgrims.

And after climbing up, I will walk downhill leaving the glaciers and clouds to enter the lush forests of the valley below. On my way down, I stop to talk to a grey-haired grandmother, her head wrapped in a dupatta, borne up on both sides by teenage grandsons, every excruciating step of the way. She had a long way to go, but her grandsons, with their barely there beards and downy moustaches, shrugged and said she had refused a pony or porter, as she had made a vow to walk – barefoot. Nearly there, I smile.

On my way down off the mountain, the sun shines, the mists clear and it turns into a glorious day. There are only a few people on the way down, and those who I met were happy to stop and chat awhile. Be warned though, that many of the teashops were already closed or closing on the way down. Maybe people don't stop on the way down, I myself want to be off the mountain and back in Ghangaria before dusk. In

SUSAN JAGANNATH

these deeply slashed valleys, dusk drops early as the sun slides behind the mountains.

Halfway down, the views of rock and gorge with free–floating clouds and pounding waterfalls are hidden by broad leafed forest, and singing birds and chirping insects interrupt the tap–tapping of poles and sticks. I was alone and yet not alone, with pilgrims and trekkers from all over stopping for a quick hello and goodbye.

Ghangaria arrives too soon, I'm happy to have made it down early – so I wander into the gurudwara there to have a look around, it is a large and spacious campus, with dorms, langar (food hall), private rooms, and of course a gurudwara where the reading of the Guru Granth Sahib is continuous.

THE GHANGARIA GURUDWARA

I sit in silence on a bright carpet and listen to the sound–why is it familiar? It is on the edge of memory – and why do I feel a wash of sadness?

Then the glossy fronds of a hand–held fan swish over the Guru Granth Sahib, and in a flash, I recall the small gurud-wara in the army unit in the backwoods of Kashmir. There weren't too many places to play in an army camp in the field.

The soldiers frowned on us climbing the tents and sliding down the sides of their tents, and there were no offenders locked up in the guardroom for us to gawk at. But the priest in the gurudwara with the soft blue carpet always had a smile and sweets for us. Then one day he went off to a forward base to perform a Guru Granth Sahib reading, and a rocket from across the border flattened the tent where the service was being held. I learned early that death could take away good people. I rise and leave, as if I could leave the memory behind in the gurudwara.

Outside the gurudwara, the street *dhabas* tempt me with fresh fried *samosas*, hot crispy saffron *jelabis* and vast vats of creamy *rabri* simmering in the stuttering light of a solar lamp. I breathe it in deeply, despite the slight oily overtones, it was good to be alive.

I pass our hotel and continue down to the massage parlor, to sit in the chairs that pummel sore feet and clutch at aching calves, a bubbling fragrant hot spa bath would be perfect, but the bubbling brooks here are those tumbling down over boulder filled valley floors

CHAPTER 15
SAUNTERINGS
IN A HOLY LAND

> *Saunter – from Saint Terre, walking to the Holy Land*
>
> *— Linguist*

This was the rest day that I thought I didn't need. Later on, I realize that a rest day between every walking day would have made the trek a better experience, a reverence to these sacred lands.

The trek had been harder, longer and higher than I expected. Assumptions had fallen by the wayside, especially the phantom of fitness. Fitness is two edged – mental and physical and one impacts the other – the obvious shortfall of physical fitness for a high–altitude climb had impacted my emotional fitness – so a day idly wandering around Ghangaria was just right.

Leaning from the balcony of the hotel, I wave to the cavalcade of mules, porters and pilgrims heading out to the valley – but for us it is a saunter down to a restaurant that offered a late south Indian breakfast. I need a break from *aloo paratha*. Fortified with not–too–fluffy idlis I wander down the lane heading valley–wards, this time browsing the shops with books and souvenirs, and checking out the other hotels.

From Ghangaria the steep black–sided gorges part to reveal a snow speckled Kamet with necklaces of glaciers. A far thatch of emerald green is the upper Valley of Flowers. But the heights are not for me today, a walk in a gentle valley by Ghangaria reveals a hidden treasure of woods, flowers and a bubbling brook, crossed by wobbly stepping stones.

MEETING AGAIN

Today is not a boot day, trainers make my feet feel light and airy – as I head into the gurudwara for a five–minute meditation. Coming out, I'm accosted by a posse of grey–haired grannies. There's no escape from a twenty–minute interrogation by curious village *Nanis* and *Dadis* (Grannies). No personal space here. They're from Ludhiana, a woolen clothing center of Punjab, but their own "sweaters" are exquisitely hand–knitted.

The grannies urge me to come again next year, and not "waste money" on hotels and restaurants.

Stay in the Gurudwara, they say, private rooms with attached bathroom and "geysers" aka small hot water boilers.

Despite the lack of mountain views, it is airy and clean, and uncrowded, at least now, as most of the pilgrims are trudging up to Hemkund Sahib.

My breathless friend from the day before comes rushing over to hug me and introduce me to more of her family and friends, rattling on rapidly in pure Punjabi. All the women are in full make—up. My face feels naked with only moisturizer and lip balm. Full marks to them for hiking in makeup from foundation to eyeshadow and lipstick, though with their dark flashing eyes and clear skin flushed a faint pink, they needed no enhancements.

I nod and smile. *Sat Sri Akaal* is 80% of my Punjabi. The other 20% is swear words probably not suitable for these sacred precincts. With a final hug and wave, she sets off back down to Gobind Ghat and her own tortured reality. I say a little prayer that she will be re—united with her children.

BERRY TASTING IN THE MEADOW

The rusty rails of the metal bridge over the Laxman Ganga are still damp with the dew and I'm loath to trust them. Nothing can resist the icy hand of winter here, and the many fallen over railings on the paths above are a warning not to lean too heavily on these railings. The triple waterfall pounds down to the creek, and the glacier has melted to a rock and pebble encrusted snow cave. Ice melt ripples out in multiple shining rivulets to join the stream, butterflies and tiny birds flit from rock to rock, flying specks of feather and sound.

Off the bridge and the main track, an overgrown path winds through the undergrowth, and stepping over some mule dung we push through the trees and bushes to the meadow beside the rock—strewn river bed. This is the unheralded confluence of the Pushpavati and Laxman Ganga, where the mountain source streams become the Bhyundar Ganga that tumbles downhill to join the Vishnu Ganga, a tributary of the Alak-nanda, that eventually becomes the Ganga. Everything is connected. High up a huge Himalayan bird floats motionless on outspread wings. At this height I can't identify whether it's an eagle or a vulture.

The meadow is dotted with flowers, an abundance of pink Himalayan balsam, red and blue Wallich geraniums and overhead on the bushes are red ripening barberry, a sour vitamin-rich berry. The guide encourages us to pluck the berries. We roll them over our fingers and taste with a tentative nibble. I wince at the extreme sourness.

I climb down to the riverbed, from boulder to boulder until we reach the sandy banks, and then wobble over the watercourses on stepping stones that threaten to tip the unwary into the water. From the far side, Ghangaria from looks picturesque from this different angle. The mountains tower overhead, it's easy to see how the snow and ice fill the narrow valley in the eight-month winter.

Pale blue waters tumble over rocks and pebbles, and the mountain is a sheer wall in front, but we wander in the idyllic flower-scented meadows cupped in a wide curve of the expanding river. A cow moos a warning, and we see it, a calf hidden in the tall Himalayan balsam. I make a quick retreat, there is plenty of room in the meadow for both of us. I have no wish for a third cow episode. My friend doesn't laugh too hard when I tell her cows kill more people a year than sharks, we're both thinking of Vibha's close encounter of the bovine kind on the way up.

I squint at a bird that wheels high above the cliffs and gorges, but is too high. I hope it's a Himalayan griffon, a type of eagle. Lower down, tinier birds flit about the valley floor, skimming the river surface, and alighting on the water splashed rocks. There may be trout in the waters, but I saw no one fishing in the streams here.

Post monsoon with less rain and lower temperatures, the river may run quiet, slipping between the boulders or gliding over the rocks. But now there are plenty of miniature waterfalls to splash in, and as the fine rain clears, a rainbow glitters over the valley and there is no one there to view it except us. Relaxing in the meadow, we talk of many things, of how to capture this moment in dance, song, picture or words and forget the world of work and busyness.

THE "HALLYPAD"

Dusting off golden flecks of pollen, we pick up our backpacks and head downstream to emerge at the far end of Ghangaria, where the lower meadows host an encampment of tents rivalling a Mughal army on the move. Row upon row of "Swiss" tents masquerade as luxury destinations for tourists, overlooking the helipad. By day there would be no mountain quiet here with the continuous buzz of the helicopters.

We stroll down to the helipad, labelled as the "Hallypad", as a tiny chopper buzzes down the valley and lands in a noisy whir of blades, the passengers scramble out, their baggage flung out and dragged away, and in a moment outgoing passengers dash out to clamber in clutching their bags. Total turn around – less than 7 minutes. A single controller with a scarf round his head and a handheld radio guides the chopper in and out, and in a nearby tent, passengers wait to show identification, pay their money and enter their names on the manifest.

THE ALCHEMISTRY OF THE HIMALAYAS

Perched on the edge of a culvert, we chat to a quad of brawny *palki* or palanquin bearers as they wait for a customer. Too late in the day to heft the *palki* up to the Valley of flowers or Hemkund, their best hope is a helicopter passenger who is too weak or old to walk even the 1 kilometer from here to Ghangaria. Four young men up from the plains of Uttar

Pradesh, they hire the *palki* from a *baniya* in Gobind Ghat for the season, and must pay him 50% of their daily take. I do a quick calculation, with a fee of Rs 8000 for the trip, means that they each make about Rs. 1000 per back-breaking trip. There is no other work in their villages they say.

On the way into Ghangaria, the conifer – lined path pools into a bay full of tethered mules, standing with heads drooping towards the grassy floor, flicking their tails at flies and mosquitoes. Beyond the track, deeper into the forest, thick stands of Himalayan pine block the sun, allowing inter-mittent pools of sunlight where blossoms cluster on mossy rocks or push through rich layers of pine needle mulch. Fallen giants, tree trunks lie prostrate along the path, covered in green velvety moss, and crumbling slowly into the earth. Deeper in the grove, lichens hang like tattered banners, flash silver in a vagrant ray of the sun, turning from tattered rag to silver gauze.

The pounding of a helicopter punctuates the Himalayan air and we turn around to pelt down to the helipad, just in time to see the helicopter land and then take off again. Like a mechanical dragonfly, it flits between the walls of the valley, just above the tree line, along the twisting course of the river, and vanishes as it's sprayed by nameless waterfalls.

And we are back to people watching, and dog watching. A massive dark dog sits alert and still by the side of the road, his tongue lolling out, waiting, expectation in every blink of his shining eyes. He never moves, once in a while his furry tail pulses on the ground, but in all the time we were there, no one came up that made him leap up in greeting. Who was he? a shepherd's dog waiting for his master to return with a flock of sheep or goats for him to chivvy along in the meadow? Or was he Yudhistra's dog, waiting for his master to return with his ticket to heaven, the only dog permitted into the divine realms in mythology. [1]

NO MORE SHEEP AND GOATS

The valley is forbidden to its original summer denizens, the herds of sheep and goats. There is no longer even goat milk available here. The sturdy shepherds selling goat milk, a feature in Frank Smythe's books are long gone.

In the eco center, a local says that almost no one in the village farms or herds sheep anymore, the revenue from the tourists and pilgrims is enough.

I feel guilt. Is this better or worse? With our need to see the world have we destroyed their way of life? The eco center is a treasure of books, maps, brochures, and CDs to learn about the flowers and wildlife of the area. And a collapsed roof on one of the buildings. A sign that the temporary settlement can be wiped out in the winter when the heavy snowfall turns to ice that grinds down mountains, rocks and buildings.

Near the tent encampment, is a tiny army company base. Barbed wire and hand–painted notices warn us to stay out of a shed with an outdoor dining area and cottages – accommodation for military personnel. It is the army engineers who originally hacked the road up to Hemkund and built both gurdwaras. Today the road is rebuilt every summer by pilgrims doing "*kar seva*" or volunteer service; but much of the engineering skill is still supplied by army units.

The Hemkund devotion is a relative newcomer to the pilgrimage circuit; the ancient site identified by an army engineer less than a century ago, appropriate for Sikhism, a young religion in India's hoary past.

A string of tired mules stumbles up the last switchback aided by shouts and flicks of rope by their handlers, laden with sheets of corrugated tin to repair roofs or build walls in the all too brief summer.

SAUNTERING IN PLACE

We saunter back, an idle day is a gift to myself. A holiday within a holiday. I wonder if I should have returned for another day in the valley – but my lungs appreciate the rest from high altitude exertions, and my stomach is on edge. I must walk down the trail to Gobind Ghat tomorrow, and the thought of a runny Delhi belly terrifies me.

The massage parlor is empty, and we plonk into chairs and foot machines. I've done no walking today, but my Fitbit indicates 5 kms today. Conscience assuaged, I continue with the foot massage. Why do I need an excuse? In the mountains, are we finding ourselves or leaving the excuses behind? When walking, everything slows down even our goldfish attention spans lengthen. Maybe our minds were built to think at the speed of a steady walk, to pay attention and learn at a deeper level. We became human when our ancestors stood up off the forest floor and reached for the sky, and the far horizons.

An animated if wilted group of women of all shapes and sizes tramp up in identical maroon t–shirts and black hiking shoes. What's their story? They decided to have an adventure, they laugh, bending down to catch their breath. Training together all year on the hot flat roads and sketchy parks of their small town, they ordered their hiking gear from Decathlon online. They've booked transport and accommodation online, and now are here. They shake their heads when I tell them they can't make the Valley of Flowers today. They think it's just a couple of kms further and it can be a short pre–dinner walk after they freshen up. What does Aunty–jee know?

No, we say, it's not possible, the forest rangers will not even let you in. Come on in, have a massage, acclimatize, rest and continue tomorrow.

The Valley of Flowers and Hemkund treks are brutal hikes complete with altitude sickness, breathlessness, exhaustion and brain freeze. The best thing is to rest after the walk from Pulna. Because both the Valley and Hemkund give you one shot to reach your destination. Once you start you must keep going, or turn back.

CHAPTER 16
THE RETURN
FLY OR WALK

> *Now shall I walk or shall I ride?*
> *'Ride,' Pleasure said;*
> *'Walk,' Joy replied."*
> *– W.H. Davies*

The end of the hike had crept up unwanted and unannounced. Time to pack up and leave – with a lot of damp clothes, but on this trek, I do not have to lug a back-pack. We hand them over to the porters to load up on the hired mules and forget about them, knowing that we will find them in Pulna. The bridge at Bhyundar has been repaired, so no need to arrange trans–shipment. I'm free to walk unen-cumbered.

Is there a greater blessing for a trek, and for life?

Trooping down for the last breakfast of the day, we will miss this morning breakfast march. This time there is no 'packed lunch' for collection. Earlier, with Delhi Belly threatening havoc, I resolved to take the helicopter ride with Vibha and the rest of the party set out to walk or ride down later. We have to hurry to be first in the queue.

A FLYING START

I munch down a couple of tiny triangles of dry toast, skip the tea, and scurry down to the booking tent. There is already a long queue, and I calculate a four-hour wait at the least. It promises to be a clear day, and my stomach seems to have settled with a half day and night of starvation and dry toast.

With a hug and a wave, I leave Vibha in the queue and walk, at what I imagine is a brisk pace.

I turn at the sound of my name, as with big smiles and triumphant waves, Anju and Shanti catch up with me, we walk together for some time − then I let them stride on on ahead, they turn and slice the air with their poles and I am alone with my trekking poles. Pilgrims stream down, with a few early starters coming up on mules.

Walking on down, poles clicking and moving between sunshine and shade, the sorrow of leaving lifts with each step; not only by the joy of tumbling waterfalls and still blooming flowers, but with movement. We are built to move, not sit around and mope. People walking up glance at me with envy, the initial bounce has been pounded out of them by the relentless climb. The downhill walk is still fraught with potential for trips, falls and encounters with blundering bovines, I hope that cow stays home today.

The path unravels through the resin scented pines, and before you know it, I hear the roar of the confluence down at the Bhyundar village and across the river at the tea shop Shanti and Anju wave encouraging mugs of tea at me.

I lean over the railing of the concrete bridge and say a silent goodbye to the torrent. As the path continues downhill, the river drops away suddenly. The vegetation changes in slow motion, 11 kilometers of downhill over cobbled stones is a long way. Why are Roman roads lauded for swift movement of those Roman legionaries marching in their sandals. In hiking boots I'm not fast, and even downhill I get breathless.

BREATHE EASY

But yes, the air is thicker now, and I breathe easier. The vegetation is lush and green, and the waterfalls now tower over helicopters that are pumping up and down the winding valley. I wave madly when they pass by with a whump whump whump, not knowing or caring if anyone is looking. Does it matter?

I wave to helicopters, pat mules as they pass, and cheer up hikers walking upwards. At the ten–kilometer mark, a despairing question, is it all uphill like this? Yes, all the way and steeper, take a mule, you haven't even begun the real climb.

No, I didn't tell her that.

But maybe I should have, do I destroy her dreams? Or let her learn the lesson in humility that I learnt? The Himalayas are great for learning by doing, by slipping, by falling and if you still don't get it, by thinning off the air so you have you have to gasp for every shred of oxygen.

The sun burns hotter and we are down at the floor of the Bhyundar valley, almost there. A cheer goes up as I around the corner, I'm the last of our group. We pose for photos, and then, it's nearly over. But we still have to collect our helicopter borne Vibha from Gobind Ghat.

At Pulna, I crush into the front seat of a shared taxi, the promise of carsickness enough to ensure me a front seat as we rattle and unspool down the last four kms to Gobind Ghat. The number of people and existence of cars and trucks astonishes, a rude awakening back to "civilization". With a series of pings, our phones come to life again, like sleeping creatures squeaking awake, prodded by an invisible harpoon.

Vibha is found, all fresh and cheerful after her helicopter 'trek'. We crowd round her phone to see the video of the four-minute flight, double delights for us. Before we can call, Happy, our taxi driver is there

I brace for more "hard" quizzes on arcane points of mythology. After all, we are on our way to the temple of Badrinath. The lodestone of Vaishnavite Hinduism.[1] There are also hot springs at Badrinath, and we talk longingly of plunging our feet into those, despite Happyji's chidings that we should be reverently waiting for *darshan* at the temple.

WHAT THE RAIN DECIDES

The rain sets in, and we press onwards to Badrinath, rolling up the windows and the windscreen wipers swishing ever faster. Traffic crawls but we continue—until the road is covered with a landslide of truck-sized boulders and slippery slush. Happy makes a captain's call and swings the car around, there will be no Badrinath today.

Instead, we head back to Auli for a late lunch, with a stop at thunderous Vishnuprayag. I descend steep stairs down to the temple where the Vishnu Ganga and the Dhauliganga converge with a thunderous roar to form the Alaknanda, one of the two source streams of the Ganges. In a deep gorge slashed into the mountains, I feel as if the entire gorge shivers with the power of Shiva letting down his hair to allow the Ganges to descend safely to earth from her home, the Milky Way in the heavens. Looking up, the sky is a narrow slot between the walls of the dark gorges. The spray mists my face with a gentle caress,

The Alaknanda punches it way down through deep gorges until at Kalpnath the gorge expands to a narrow green fringed valley. Brown and churning, rolling rocks down in the monsoon, in the winter the Alaknanda transforms into a liquid turquoise stream. But for now, we climb again, back up the precipitous stairs, breathless on our way to the road and taxi.

We're on the last stretch to Auli, via Joshimath where we are back in small town India. Joshimath has been a pilgrimage town for hundreds of years, the winter home of the priests of Badrinath. The old part of the town with narrow winding streets, and the urban sprawl is brutalistic concrete nouveau India, with steel poles sticking out of the roofs, where owners plan yet another precarious level.

RICE AND RAJMA WITH A DASH OF LIME

Happy pulls up on a narrow street and directs us up a steep flight of stairs. They lead us up to a double-glass door of a plush restaurant perched on the edge of a slope, called Food Plaza. A sudden thirst assails us and while we wait for everyone to gather there from toilet visits and ATM visits, I order fresh lime soda after fresh lime soda – I opt for soda to avoid drinking water, hoping that it is cleaner than tap water. The clean sharp taste of fresh lime soda with sugar and salt is the taste of a hundred summer evenings at home, sitting under the bright stars of a North Indian sky, because it was too hot to stay inside a home that still radiated the heat of a summer day.

The long wait convinces me that there is only one person in the entire Food plaza. We ask the nervous waiter for multiple dishes from the menu, interested in some carnivorous option after our forced vegetarianism, and in fits and starts, word comes back from the kitchen:

- No mutton (goat meat)
- No chicken
- No eggs

We settle for a local dish that we haven't eaten as yet, as none us can look a *paratha* in the eye for some time. I wait for the message to come back – but the dishes come out and we fall on our repast of *rajma* (red kidney beans) and rice. It is rare to find local food here, it appears as if all the food outlets cater to Punjabis and South Indians.

The temple priests here have been South Indian Brahmins for many generations. I wonder what happened to the local priests over the centuries.

Adi Shankaracharya, the South Indian reformer led a great Hindu push against Buddhism in the 6th Century A.D. It highlights the power of story, as he retold the ancient myths and situated them in real places right here in the Himalayas. Believers preferred the rich palette of a story, rather than the austere intellectualism of Buddhism.

CHAPTER 17
THE GODDESS REVEALED
WISDOM

> *I have no idea where I am going.*
>
> *I do not see the road ahead of me.*
>
> *I will not fear, for you are ever with me,*
>
> *and you will never leave me to face my perils alone.*
>
> — *Thomas Merton Prayer*

Escaping the grimy suburbs of Joshimath, we pass the neat cantonment areas, with acres of olive–green trucks parked in military precision. Then higher still are apple orchards heavy with fruit. Nearer Auli, we pass army trucks and buses full of smartly uniformed school kids on their way home. A few decades ago, I was one of these. For two magical years we lived in the vale of Kashmir among the blossoms of almond trees in spring, and snowy field in the winters. The summers were spent fishing in innumerable crystal streams bubbling down from the mountains. And school days were appended with long rides home in just such olive – green buses.

ONE LAST EVENING

We arrive, and again, those steep broken steps, but we have one last evening and night of breathtaking views from Nandadevi to Kamet, and Neelkanth and Mana. So far we haven't had an unimpeded view of Nanda Devi, the giver of peace and contentment. Local legend says that the clouds are from the kitchen of the goddess. The devi has been cooking up a storm these last few days then.

After the mandatory climb up the steep and broken stairs we find the retired botanists strolling downhill – their guide had taken them up to the cable car start, and walked them down from there. Maybe our guide doesn't like us much – who knows? At the end of our tour, the indifferent hotel staff at Auli ignore us. And we them.

We make ourselves teabag tea in the rooms, and bring out our cups to lounge on the plastic chairs on the verandahs drinking in the magnificence of mountains.

A last evening in this mountain eyrie, spending time with new and old friends and a rush out for hot water. And then it's time to pack in readiness for our exit in the morning. And the last chance for photos and fervent promises to return in the winter.

MORNING BENEDICTION

The morning dawns clear and the mountains gleam a rosy pink in the morning sun. The peaks encircle us in a glimmering embrace and far to the north west, the clouds finally part, like a bride drawing her veil, Nanda Devi floats into full vision – the blessing of the goddess herself. We're all daughters of the Himalayas, culturally, physically and emotionally, and are drawn back to gaze upon her, in *Darshan*. Leave a blessing as you pass.

With a last longing glance at the flower—studded alpine meadows above Auli, it's time to begin the long drive to Haridwar. A long drive, but with a brilliant day, the driver chuckles that we will be in Haridwar by 2 pm.

But before that there is one more temple to be visited on this mountain, and it can only be approached on foot.

A SLICE OF THE SOUTH

Adi Shankaracharya came up here from South India, more than a millennium ago— and the Vridha Badri temple was established by him in the 8th Century. We leave the road at an arched pathway, on a downhill trek to the temple. At Animath village there is no road. Instead, we walk down stone flagged paths fringed with fresh green pumpkin creepers, between shale—roofed homes with wooden balconies perched precariously at the side. The only thing separating us from ageless views are the solar panels that line the path.

In a stone walled paddock, a rusty brown cow and golden calf blink gently at us, obviously well cared for and tethered to a firm pole. I like this kind of safe cow.

Stepping left off the road we enfilade between lush green paddies, where a man and woman are cutting the rice. It's not harvest season, so we wonder and ask. The rice plants are being trimmed and the tops of the plants being used as fodder for the cows and goats. Nothing is wasted here, and here at the end of the monsoon, the villagers are already readying for winter. Above the field's bare slopes of rock climb upwards into misty cloud, and on the far side tiny villages cling limpet—like to steep mountainsides.

The Vridha Badri temple, nestles beneath a giant banyan tree, and looking beyond the garish tarpaulin, the ancient crumbling stone edifice peers out from a turmeric washed closet lit by flickering *diyas*, earthenware lamps. Pots of crinkly petalled marigold bloom amidst the pumpkin creeper invasion. The original idol of Vishnu as an old man that appeared here is now in the Badrinath temple. So even though landslides prevented us from visiting Badrinath, we do have *darshan* here. We ring the bell, and say a goodbye.

After a slight detour as we wander in the wrong direction, the woman in the paddy field directs us to the correct path, and we loiter on our way down to where Happy and the taxi wait to bear us away to Haridwar. Happyji as you may have guessed by now, is deeply concerned about our spiritual needs, and decrees that we visit the temple at Rudraprayag, where the Mandakini joins the Alaknanda.

Fortunately for us, the highway overlooks the confluence and town, and obviously, there are other weary pilgrims who would like to see the temple from above. Inverting human and divine, we look down at a miniature temple dwarfed by the mountains.

At Kaudiyala, we stop at a tourist department cafeteria – Daniel's Dip. I remember rafting past this a few years ago on the rapids called by the same name. Where a pristine beach once was, a series of wooden cabins line the bank overlooking the river separated by emerald lawns, and a disinterested staff serve us tea and pakoras. The rapids are barely visible today, the rush of monsoonal water covers them. This is a popular stretch for kayaking and white-water rafting – but not in the monsoon, there is just too much water. I sip the tea and look at the water, remembering the icy water welling up around our toes, and the frantic paddling as we negotiated the rapids, airborne for at least half the way as the raft lifts high and slaps back down on the water with a thud.

HOLY HARIDWAR

We are on the last stretch back to Haridwar, and ahead of us we see long lines of traffic – more landslides and roadworks delay us for hours.

Finally, we rush past Rishikesh, and head into Haridwar at dusk. We may be late, but nothing will stop us from the last temple, and the last treat we have planned – street food, chaat and puris in the teeming pilgrim markets behind the temple. But first we have to get to Har ki Podi at the exact spot where the Ganges enters the plains.

We dump our baggage at the hotel, and make our way down teeming road towards the temples.

It is a grey grimy dusk until the temples light up, the many hues floating above the darkened ghats, and the precinct transforms into a magic fairyland of gleaming domes beside the swift flowing waters of the Ganges.

We remove our shoes and tip toe silently down the steps into the chill of the water to receive a last blessing from the holy river. It is done.

PART IV

Reference Guide

APPENDIX A

PACKING LIST

Make sure you bring enough clothes, as wet clothes will not dry easily.

- 6–8 tops
- 4–5 trousers, leggings or cargo pants
- A warm jacket
- A sun hat
- A beanie or warm cap
- Slippers to use in the bathroom
- Flat shoes for the evenings
- A small flashlight or headlamp
- Sunscreen
- Water bottle
- First aid kit including medication such as Diamox, Roko etc for stomach upsets
- Insect repellent
- A pair of small towels
- Plastic bags to protect your electronic items, I had a number of zip lock bags
- Plastic bags to protect your backpacks, and shoes, as

well as to carry your disposable masks, gloves and other trash away

- Trail mix to munch on the way, protein bars and chocolate
- Trekking poles
- ID such as Aadhar or Passport, 2 passport sized photos
- Oxygen can
- Sleeping bag and sleeping bag liner
- Sheets and pillows
- Fitness Tracker
- Phone with Indian SIM
- Camera—with extra SD cards, if you don't want to use your phone
- Batteries for phone/camera/Go Pro
- Selfie stick
- Chargers for all your equipment, with converters for Indian electrical points. A small expander board to charge all your equipment
- Electric power adapter for India. (220 volts and at 50 Hertz)
- USB Chargers for India
- Rain gear to keep you waterproof; poncho that you can throw over everything for light drizzles; rain jacket with hood and rain pants for heavier downpours
- Chaps to protect your boots and lower half of trousers
- Six sets of underwear
- A scarf, both for cooler days and to wear in the evenings, in a complementary color
- One jacket or jumper for the evenings.
- Socks, socks, socks! 6 pairs of sock sets (a set is one thinner one, and one thicker one, that you wear at all

times). Do not stint on socks; take a couple of extra pairs if necessary. You can even change socks in the middle of a day of walking. Keep your feet dry and clean

- One set of warm merino inners, top and bottom (I used this to sleep in)
- ½–litre water bottle: This is absolutely essential
- Masks, at least two for each day
- Disposable gloves
- Food containers to carry your food, and eat from. These are called "tiffins" or "tiffin boxes" Tupperware will do, as well.
- A small flask to keep hot beverages, such as tea.
- A drinking glass or cup
- Cutlery
- Lock and key to lock your room
- Pens and pencils.

NICE TO HAVE

- A small notebook, marker pen, and Post–it notes.
- A 10–day supply of any vitamins and supplements or medicines that you need: Double up on fish oil and vitamins and glucosamine when walking to maintain optimal fitness.
- Two pocket pack of tissues in case of sniffles.
- Six handkerchiefs of the quick–drying kind: You need this to wipe your face, back of your neck, and any other damp parts.

TOILETRIES

- Disinfectant wipes
- Dettol or other disinfectant
- Toothbrush and paste
- Shampoo in the small travel–size pack, or any sample sachets that you may have got as free samples (use it as soap as well)
- Vaseline or any lubricating cream
- Moisturizer, night cream, etc. in small packs or sachets
- Women's sanitary products such as tampons or pads plus disposal bags
- Small zip lock bag so that you can keep them all together
- Nail clippers and small scissors
- Medicine or first aid kit
- Blister medicine or strips
- Band–Aids in all sizes
- Panadol or Ibuprofen, one strip (you can buy more in any chemist if necessary)
- Vicks VapoRub (I used this on my feet every day)
- Cough lozenges, one strip
- Sunscreen, small
- Insect repellent, small
- Stingose or any other cream to soothe insect bites
- Pressure bandages, knee brace, etc. in case of falls or trips
- Toilet paper, one roll for emergencies: (Zip lock bags to carry this away and dump in the nearest trash bin. Please do not litter the mountains)
- Emergency repair kits

You never know when you will need these:

- Needle and thread
- Glue for emergency shoe repairs
- Nappy pins
- Duct tape or cello tape
- Sticker labels
- A set of carabiners of different sizes, so that you can safely clip various things outside your backpack.

Tip: Pack everything in zip lock bags, labeled so that you can repack and find things quickly, and to protect from rain.

BACKUPS

An encrypted USB drive with:

- Copies of the first page of your passport, and any pages with visas on them
- Travel itinerary
- Hotel bookings
- Medical insurance
- A page with your credit card numbers, passport numbers, etc.
- Phone numbers of your financial institution, embassy numbers, etc.
- Also put this list up on your Dropbox, or Google Drive, so that you can access it online if you lose the USB drive.

APPENDIX B

SHRI HEMKUND SAHIB TRUST

In the gurudwaras pilgrims can stay in the "hall" (dormitories) or in s private room if available. Simple vegetarian food is served in the *Langar* (Food) hall and most have simple medical facilities. Accommodation is open for all regardless of faith, class or caste.

Rishikesh Gurudwara

Address: Chauda Bigha, Chandreshwar Nagar, Rishikesh, Uttarakhand 249137

Google Map Location – **http://bit.ly/2maiyIR Srinagar Gurudwara**

Address – Srinagar–Badrinath Highway, gola bazar, Rawadi, Uttarakhand 246174

Google Map Location – **http://bit.ly/2klFzSu**

Joshimath Gurudwara

Address – Joshimath, Uttarakhand 246443

Google Map Location – **http://bit.ly/2mivIon**

Gurudwara Gobind Ghat

Address: Chamoli, Uttarakhand 246443

GARHWAL ACCOMMODATION IN GOVERNMENT GUESTHOUSES

GMVN Help Line NO

0135– 2746817, 2749308

+91 9568006639

info@gmvnl.in

https://www.gmvnonline.com/

https://www.gmvnonline.com/accommodations

Auli – AULI (Cloud End and Nanda Devi Eco Resort

01389–223208, 01389–223305, 9568006629 (M)

Joshimath (Jyothir Tourist Complex)

01389–222226, 9568006667 (M)

Nandprayag (Nanda Tourist Complex)

01372–261215, 9568006676 (M)

Gwaldam

9568006660 (M)

Haridwar (Rahi Motel)

01334–226430, 01334–228686, 9568006661 (M)

Kaudiyala

01378–262911

Rishikesh (Ganga Resort)

0135–2438651, 9568006683 (M)

HOMESTAYS IN THE VICINITY

https://www.peachesandpears.net/

APPENDIX C

TRANSPORT AND OTHER

POLICE

https://www.facebook.com/uttarakhandpolice/

BUS SERVICES

https://www.utconline.uk.gov.in/

HELICOPTER SERVICES

https://www.sacredyatra.com/chardham–helicopter–service–status.html

TAXI – HAPPY'S CHAR DHAM

+91 94120 71345

+91 76684 36020

email: Chardhamwithhappy@gmail.com

APPENDIX D
GLOSSARY

Aarti – Worship service with lamps.

Aloo paratha – Flat bread with spiced potato stuffing.

Baman Daur – Boulder Gate.

Baniya – Merchant.

Bugyal – Alpine meadow.

Biriyani – Spiced rice with vegetables and/or meat.

Chaat – Spicy street food snacks.

Chai – Tea.

Chillas – Gluten-free flat breads.

Chitti – Letter or ticket

Cheenti – Ants.

Chinti – Sprinkle water.

Chota Char Dham – Four sacred sites in the Himalayas.

Darshan – The act of seeing.

Darzee – Tailor.

Dekchi – Cooking pot.

Devi – Goddess

Dhaba – Roadside restaurant.

Dhal – A lentil soup.

Dwari Pairi – Fairy Gate.

Dupatta – A scarf.

Dadi – Paternal grandmother.

Gulab Jamun – Sweet fried dumpling soaked in syrup.

Gurudwara – Sikh temple.

Gura–ka–langar – Free food in a Sikh temple.

Ghee – Rendered butter.

Idli – Steamed rice dumpling.

Jo Bole so Nihal – The Pure One Says

Jawan – a soldier in the Indian army.

Jelabi – A sticky orange sweet.

Kathak – Classical North Indian Dance.

Kar Seva – Free service.

Khachad – Mule.

Keechad – Wet sticky mud.

Khichdi – Rice and dal, similar to a risotto

Khud – The downhill part of a steep valley.

Kohinoor – Fabled diamond of the Mughals, now in the British Crown.

Kulcha – Tandoori roti.

Matha-jee - Respected Mother

Maharani –Empress, Queen.

Mochi – Shoemaker.

Masala – Spice.

Nani – Maternal grandmo.ther.

Nullah – Storm water drain.

Pakoras – Fried spicy dumpling snacks.

Palki – Palanquin.

Parathas – Flat bread cooked with a little oil.

Parikrama – Circuit around a sacred site.

Pittoowallah or Pittoo – Porter with Basket

Pind – Village, typically in the Punjab.

Ponywallah - Muleteer.

Prayag – River confluence.

Puja –Worship.

Pujari – Temple priest.

Puri – Fried breads.

Rasagulla – Steamed milk dumplings soaked in sugar syrup.

Rabri – Milk and rice pudding.

Rajma – Red Kidney beans.

Razai – Quilt.

Roti – Flatbread, or any bread.

Rogan Josh – A meat curry.

Sat Sri Akaal – The One Lord is True.

Sabji – Vegetable, either raw, or cooked.

Sanyas – Retire from worldly life.

Shudh – Pure.

Tandoori Tikka – Kebab meat baked in an oven.

Thali – Plate.

Topi – Hat.

PART V

Brief Reference Guide to the Flowers

APPENDIX E
LIST OF BLUE FLOWERS

A short list of the commonly found blue flowers.

All plants in the Valley of Flowers National Park are protected by law, do not pluck or destroy any part of the plant.

More information and photographs here:

https://susanjagannath.com/vof-bonus/

Aconitum balfourii, Indian Aconite, Meetha Vish, Mintha

Botanical Family: Ranunculaceae or Buttercup.

When: Flowers in Late August to mid September.

Occurrence: Near Baman Daur

Status: Rare Endangered species

Note: Tuberous roots of Aconitum balfourii Stapf are rich sources of pseudoaconitine (0.4 to 0.5%) and aconite alkaloids, used particularly in Homeopathy, Ayurveda, and Unani systems of medicine.

Aconitum Violaceum, Indian Aconite, Kadwi

Botanical Family: Ranunculaceae

When: Mid September

Occurrence: Hemkund Sahib Lake and on the way to Hemkund Sahib

Note: All parts of the plant are highly poisonous. The plant is used as narcotic and for scorpion bites. Also known as Monkshood or Wolfsbane.

Blue Poppy, Meconopsis Aculeata, Neela Posta

Botanical Family: Papaveraceae.

When: Flowering time June to September.

Occurrence: Hemkund Sahib in first half of August.

Can sometimes be found blooming before the Dwairi Pari after the entry gate of Valley of Flowers.

Status: Rare Endangered species

Note: This is not a poppy at all, but Meconopsis means "like a poppy". While the whole plant i was used as a tonic, the roots are poisonous.

Cynanthus Microphyllus, Small–leaved Trailing Bellflower

Botanical Family: Campanulaceae (Bellflower family)

When: August to October. A late flowering plant.

Occurrence: In the middle of Valley of flowers, in the second zone, just after crossing first stream.

Cyananthus Lobatus, Trailing Bellflower

Botanical Family: Campanulaceae

When: June to September.

Occurrence: In the middle of Valley of flowers, in the second zone

Note: The flowers are used in Tibetan medicine, they are said to have a sweet, astringent and acrid taste with a cooling effect. They have laxative effect.

Saussurea Simpsoniana, Jogipadshah

Botanical Family: Asteraceae (Sunflower family)

When: July to October

Occurrence: Above Hemkund Sahib, high altitudes only.

Other Information: A curious plant that looks like a woolly mound. A well known medicinal plant of Kashmir where the whole plant is used in treating boils.

Corydalis Cashmeriana, Blue Corydalis, Kashmir Corydalis

Family name Fumariaceae (Fumitory Family)

When: May to September.

Occurrence: In the first zone, on the banks of the river.

Other Information: The word Corydalis is derived from Greek word Korudalos means Lark on account of the sky-blue flowers with darker tips.

Geranium Wallichianum, Ratanjot, Kaphlya, Laljar

Family name Geraniaceae (Geranium Family)

When: July to September

Occurrence: In abundance in the Valley of Flowers

Other Information: The juice of the plant is applied to fresh cuts to stem the bleeding. It is named after Nathaniel Wallich, a surgeon and botanist founder of the Indian Museum and the Calcutta Botanical Gardens.

Campanula Latifolia, Large Bellflower

Family name: Campanulaceae (Bellflower family)

When: Mid July

Occurrence: This flower is seen in huge colonies near the Baman Duar at the start of the valley.

Note: Grows in tall erect plants.

Cicerbita Macrorhiza, Violet Dandelion, Chyate

Family name: Cicerbita Wallroth

When: August to October

Occurrence: Before crossing the wooden bridge at official starting point of Valley of flowers.

Note: The word Macrorhiza derived from Macro means large and Rhiza means root stock, referring to large rootstock.

Gaultheria Trichophylla, Creeping snowberry, East wintergreen, Checkberry, Himalayan Snowberry, Bher,

Family name: Gaultheria Linnaeus

When: June to September

Occurence: After crossing a wooden bridge before the Baman Duar, climb about ten to fifteen meters to the left of the path, to see these beautiful berries hidden in leaves.

Note: The fruits are edible. Do not pluck them as they are protected.

Gentiana Pedicellata, Choti Buggi

Family name: Gentianceae (Gentian Family)

Flowering time : June to Late July

Occurrence: just beyond the Baman Dwar.

Gentiana Phyllocalyx

Family name: Gentianaceae (Gentian Family)

When: June to September.

Occurrence: Hemkund Sahib, across the lake.

Iris Kemaonensis, Balupuchhya, Lathum

Family name: Iridaceae

When: June to August

Occurence: Just ahead of the entry gate, before the river.

Notes: Roots are poisonous.

Phlomis Bracteosa, Jamtikle

Family name: Phlomis Linnaeus

When: July to August

Occurrence: On the open meadows in the main part of Valley of flowers.

Polemonium Caeruleum, Himalayanum Jacob's ladder

Family name: Polemoniaceae (Phlox Family)

When June to September

Occurence: Widespread in the Valley of Flowers in July

Note: The plant was used as a medicinal herb in ancient Greece..

Anemone obtusifolia, Himalayan Thimble, Kalkrya, Kanch Phool, Ratanjot

Family name: Anemone (Linnaeus)

When: May to early August

Occurence: Near Ghangaria and on towards Valley of flowers and Hemkund Sahib. Abundant in July.

Note: Anemone closes its petals in the evening and during the rains.

Aster Albescens, Fading Himalayan Aster, Lilac Himalayan Aster, Aster Linnaeus

Family name: Asteraceae (Sunflower Family)

When June to September

Occurence: From Ghangaria to the entry gate of Valley of flowers in the month of July.

Aster Diplostephioides, Creeping Aster

Family name: Astern (Linnaeus)

When: June to September, July and up to mid August is the best.

Occurence: At the far end of the valley of flowers on the banks of the Pushpawati River Bed. You can find it easily in the month of July and up to mid August.

Astragalus Himalayanus, Himalayan Milk Vetch, Semuel

Family name: Fabaceae (Pea Family)

When: June to August

Occurrence: About two kilometers from the entry gate.

Campanula Pallida, Pale Bellflower, Nepali Bikh

Family name: Campanulaceae (Bellflower Family)

When: June to October

Occurence: From Gobind Ghat to Ghangaria.

Note: This plant is found at an altitude of 1300 to 3000 meters.

Commelina Benghalensis, Bengal Spiderwort, Kanjula, Kansura

Family name: Commelinaceae (Spiderwort Family)

When:July to October

Occurence: From Gobind Ghat to Ghangaria

Erigeron Multiradiatus, Rayhanda

Family name: Erigeron (Linnaeus)

When: August to September

Occurrence: Widespread in the Valley, and near the entry gate in Septmber.

Lactuca Dolichophylla, Gringalik

Family name: Lactuca (Linnaeus)

When: July to October

Occurence: From Gobind Ghat to Ghangaria.

Saussurea Piptathera

Family name: Saussurea (De Candolle)

When: July to September

Occurence: On the Pusphawati River Bed in Valley of Flowers and near Hemkund Sahib Lake.

Note: This is a higher altitude flower, found at 3200–3800 m.

APPENDIX F
LIST OF YELLOW FLOWERS

A short list of the commonly found yellow flowers.

All plants in the Valley of Flowers National Park are protected by law. Do not pluck or destroy any part of the plan

More information and photographs here:

https://susanjagannath.com/vof-bonus/

Vajardanti, Potentilla agyrophylla, Himalayan Cinquefoil

Family Name: Rosaceae

When: June to August

Occurrence: Not as common as the red potentilla, but they can be found in the second zone of the Valley of Flowers.

Vajardanti, Potentilla Cuneifolia

Family Name: Rosaceae

When: June to August.

Occurrence: Not as common as the red potentilla, but they can be found in the second zone of the Valley of Flowers.

Saxifraga Brunonis

Family name: Saxifragaceae

When: June to August

Occurrence:Look for them in moist and shady places in Valley of Flowers.

Saxifraga Parnassifolia, Meconopsis Aculeata, Himalayan Saxifrage, Bog–Star Leaf Saxifrage

Family name: Saxifragaceae – Saxifrage family

When: August to October

Occurrence: At Hemkund Sahib Lake and on the way to Hemkund Sahib, occasionally you some flowers bloom near the entry gate of Valley of Flowers.

Caltha Palustris, Marsh Marigold, Shomalap

Family name: Caltha (Linaeus)

When: June to August.

Occurrence: Abundant on river banks and in damp areas.

Gagealutea, Yellow star of Bethlehem

Family name: Gagea Salisbury

When: May to June

Occurrence: Easily seen on the way to Hemkund Sahib.

Impatiens Scabrida, Bantil, Tillua, Rindliya

Family name: Balsaminaceae (Balsam)

When: June to September

Occurrence: On the trek from Gobind Ghat to Ghangaria.

Lilium Oxypetalum, Nomocharis oxypetala, Yellow Himalayan Lily

Family name: Lilium (Linnaeus)

When: Early to Mid July

Occurrence: Near the start of the valley, about 300 meters from Baman Daur.

Viola Biflora, Yellow Violet, Banfsa, Dundibirali, Vanafsa

Family name: Violaceae (Violet Family)

When: June to August

Occurrence: On the way to Gobind Ghat to Ghangaria from July to mid August.

Berberis Jaeschkeana, Barberry, Kingor

Family name: Berberidaceae (Barberry Family)

When: June to August

Occurrence: In early June it can be found near the entry gate.

Note: The plant is used as an astringent and roots are employed on cuts and wounds, used in treating skin diseases, urinary disorders and jaundice.

Ligularia Amplexicaulis

Family name: Ligularia Cassini

When: July to September

Occurrence: Ligularia Amplexicaulis can be seen at the entry gate, on both sides of the river at Dwairi Pari and onwards into the Valley of Flowers. This flower can be spotted easily from mid July to mid August.

Corydalis Cornuta, Balsam Jar, Balsam Jadi, Indra Jatta

Family name: Fumariaceae (Fumitory Family)

When: June to August

Occurrence: Near streams in Valley of Flowers and on the bank of Hemkund Sahib lake.

Cremanthodium Arnicoides, Himalayan Daisy

Family name: Cremanthodium

When: June to September

Occurrence: In the first half of Valley of Flowers, up to three kilometers from the entry gate, as well as on the way to Hemkund Sahib.

Erysimum Hieraciifolium

Family name: Erysimum

When: June to September

Occurrence: From Gobind Ghat to Ghangaria, not easily found in the Valley of the flowers.

Pedicularis Hoffmeisteri, Haldya Phool

Family name: Pedicularis (Linnaeus Lousewort)

When: July to August

Occurrence: Abundant in almost all parts of Valley of Flowers.

Rhodiola Imbricata

Family name: Rhodiola (Linnaeus)

When: June to August

Occurrence: More abundant at the higher reaches of the Hemkund Sahib trek.

Note: The plant is used for adaptogenic use, antidepressants, and anti–inflammatory remedies.

Nepeta Govaniana, Catmint

Family name: Lamiaceae

When: August to September

Occurrence: About three kilometers from the entry gate of Valley of Flowers till the official starting point of Valley of Flowers.

Senecio Laetus, Ragwort, Zerjum

Family name: Senecio (Linnaeus)

When: Mid–July to August

Occurrence: Abundant in all parts of Valley of Flowers.

Note: The entire plant is used for inflammation and sore throat.

Solidago Virgaurea, Golden Rod, Pinja–Phool, Sonali

Family name: Solidago (Linnaeus)

When: June to September

Occurrence: Can be found in damp places especially in the dense forest near the entry gate of Valley of Flowers.

Note: The whole plant is used to treat asthma.

Inula Grandiflora, Showy Inula

Family name: Inula (Linnaeus)

When: Late June to September

Occurrence: This flower is abundant for the first 2 kilometers from the entry gate.

APPENDIX G

LIST OF WHITE FLOWERS

A short list of the commonly found white flowers.

All plants in the Valley of Flowers National Park are protected by law. Do not pluck or destroy any part of the plant.

More information and photographs here:

https://susanjagannath.com/vof-bonus/

Geranium—robertianum, Herb Robert, Red Robin, Ratanjot, Kaphlya, Laljar

Family name: Geraniaceae (Geranium Family)

When: Mid July to Mid August

Occurrence: On the path from Gobind Ghat to Ghangaria

Other Information: The whole plant is used to treat toothache.

Viola Pilosa, Thungtu, Banfsha

Family name: Violaceae (Violet Family)

When: May to July

Occurrence: Near the entry gate.

Other Information: The whole plant is used in treating fevers.

Ainsliaea Aptera, Whorl Flower, Karu–Bhuti, Khad–Jhari

Family name: Asteraceae (Aster or Sun Flower Family)

When: June to July

Occurrence: In the forest at the start of the trek.

Allium Humile

Family name: Allium (Linnaeus)

When: May to July

Occurrence: On the banks of streams, on Pushpawati river bed in the Valley of Flowers.

Other Information: Allium Humile is a high altitude onion species.

Anaphalis Triplinervis, Bugla, Buglya, Bukki

Family name: Asteraceae

When: June to September

Occurrence: About two kilometers from entry gate of Valley of Flowers. It blooms early in June even before the glacier melts.

Anemone Tetrasepala, Four Sepalled Anemone

Family name: Anemone (Linnaeus)

When: June to August

Occurrence: Blooms in abundance in Valley of Flowers in late July.

Roscoea Purpurea

Family name: Roscoea (Smith)

When: June to August

Occurrence: On the trek from Gobind Ghat to Ghangaria.

Spiraea Canescens, Jhair–Mairala, Kathmantiyal

Family name: Spiraea Linnaeus

When: May to October

Occurrence: On the trek from Gobind Ghat to Ghangaria.

Halenia Elliptica, Spurred Gentian, Hasela

Family name: Halenia (Borkh)

When: July to October

Occurrence: Found near the Valley of Flowers entry gate in the month of September.

Impatiens Devendrae

Family name: Balsaminaceae (Balsam Family)

When: June to September

Occurrence: Abundant on the Gobind Ghat to Ghangaria trek, on the banks of the Pushpavati past Dwairi Pari.

Jancus Thomsonii

Family name: Juncaceae (Rush Family)

When: June to September

Occurrence: Hemkund Sahib

Leontopodium Brachyactis, Lion Foot

Family name: Leontopodium

When: June to August

Occurrence: Further part of the Valley of Flowers on grassy slopes after the Silver birch/ Bhojpatra forest.

Parnassia Nubicola, Phutkya

Family name: Parnassia (Linnaeus)

When: June to September

Occurrence: Near the entry gate of Valley of Flowers, and near the glacier on the way to the Valley of Flowers in June.

Note: The plant extract is used in the treatment of food poisoning. The extract of root–stock is applied externally in snakebite.

Prenanthes Brunoniana, Nimula

Family name: Prenanthes (Linnaeus)

When: August to Late October

Occurrence: Abundant in the main part of the Valley in the month of September.

Primula Reidii

Family name: Primula (Linnaeus)

When: June to September

Occurrence: This flower is found in small colonies on the bank of the river near the entry gate of Valley of Flowers early in the season when the river is still frozen.

Trichosanthes Tricuspindata, Indrayan

Family name: Trichosanthes (Linnaeus)

When: April to September

Occurrence: On the trek from Gobind Ghat to Ghangaria.

Polygonum Polystachyum, Himalayan Knotweed, Ama–Haldu, Durfi

Family name: Polygonum (Linnaeus)

When: July to September

Occurrence: This is a weed. It is everywhere in Valley of Flowers, and the Department works to remove it manually.

Saussurea gossypiphora, Fen Kamal

When: June to September

Occurrence: Hemkund Sahib Lake

Status: Endangered

Note: Plant is considered as sacred. The term Gossypi means cotton and Phora means bearing, referring to the cottony nature of the flower.

APPENDIX H

LIST OF RED AND PINK FLOWERS

A short list of the commonly found red and pink flowers.

All plants in the Valley of Flowers National Park are protected by law. Do not pluck or destroy any part of the plant.

More information and photographs here:

https://susanjagannath.com/vof-bonus/

Potentilla Atrisanguinea, Himalayan Cinquefoil, Vajradanti

Family name: Rosaceae

When: June to August

Occurrence: In abundance in the Valley of flowers and on the trek from about one kilometer from the entry gate.

Geranium Collinum, Pannir Soppu

Family name: Geraniaceae (Geranium Family)

When: July to August.

Occurrence: Near the Pushpawati River bed.

Primula Denticulata, Primrose, Drumstick Primula, Jalkutre

Family name: Primula

When: May to June

Occurrence: In early June near the Valley of Flowers entry gate when the river is still frozen. It blooms in huge numbers.

Other Information:The word Primula is derived from the Latin Primus meaning first, as these flowers are the first to bloom in spring.

Thymus Linearis, Linear Leaved Thyme, Balma–jhar, Ban Ajwain

Family name: Thymus

When: May to September

Occurrence: Thymus Lineris spreads over the rocks on the path inside the valley of flowers.

Note: It is a strongly scented herb.

Indigofera Heterantha, Himalayan Indigo, Kathi, Kathoj, Sakina

Family name: Indigofera Linnaeus

When: May to October

Occurrence: Between Gobind Ghat and Ghangaria.

Note: Flowers are used as a vegetable and the leaves are used as a herbal remedy for dysentery and cough.

Bistorta Affinis

Family name: Bistorta (Scopoli)

Occurrence: Near the Pushpawati river bed in Valley of flowers and on the path to Hemkund Sahib as well.

Note: The whole plant is used to treat colds and diarrhoea.

Cypripedium Himalaicum, Himalayan Venus

Family name: Cypripedium (Linnaeus)

When: July

Occurrence: This is a rare orchid found in Valley of flowers. It occurs slightly off the path before Baman Daur, you will probably need a guide to locate this flower.

Note: For the best chance to see this flower, trek in the second week of July.

Dactylorhiza Hatagirea, Hathageri, Paanch Anguli, Salaam Panja

Family name: Dactylorhiza (Necker)

When: June to August

Occurrence: On the slopes of the Valley of flowers between July to mid August.

Epilobium Latifolium, River Beauty

Family name: Onagraceae (Evening Primrose or Willow herb family)

When: July to October

Occurrence: Further into Valley of flowers on the banks of the Pushpavati. Abundant from 15th July to 15th August.

Pedicularis Porrecta

Family name: Pedicularis (Linnaeus)

When: June to August

Occurrence: Further into Valley of flowers on the banks of the Pushpavati.

Note: The word Porrecta is derived from word Porrectus means extended horizontally. Referring to the upper part of the flower.

Pedicularis Punctata

Family name: Pedicularis (Linnaeus)

When: August to October

Occurrence: While it is in various part of valley of flowers, it is more abundant further into Valley of flowers on the banks of the Pushpavati.

Rhodiola Heterodonta

Family name: Crassulaceae (Stone Corp Family)

When: June to August

Occurrence: Hemkund Sahib area, but also occurs deeper into the Valley, near Pushwapati river bed.

Rosa Macrophylla, Wild Rose, Band Gulab, Dand Kunja

Family name: Rosa (Linnaeus)

When: June to August

Occurrence: Abundant in two colours, white and pink, near the Valley of Flowers gate as well as near the Pushpawati river bed after the silver birch forest.

Alteris Pauciflora

Family name: Liliaceae (Lily or Onion Family)

When: June to July

Occurrence: A tiny flower on Pushpawati river bed in Valley of flowers and on the banks of Hemkund Sahib lake.

Morina Longifolia, Biskanakara, Biskandru

Family name: Dipsacaceae (Teasel or Scabious Family)

When: June to September

Occurrence: Blooms from from the entry gate of Valley of flowers and right up to the Pushpawati river bed at various spots. Mid July is the best time.

Rhododendron Lepidotum

Family name: Rhododendron (Linnaeus)

When: June to early August

Occurrence: On a grassy slope near the entry gate of Valley of flowers, usually in bloom until the end of July.

Aruncus Dioicus, Goat's beard or Bride's feathers

Family name: Rosaceae (Rose Family)

When: July to August

Occurrence: About a kilometer from the entry gate on both sides of the path.

Colquhounia Coccinea, Himalayan Mint Shrub

Family name: Lamiaceae (Mint Family)

When: August to September

Occurrence: On the path from Gobind Ghat to Ghangaria. The mules love to nibble on this plant

Impatiens Sulcata, Dog Flower, Chaul, Kwal

Family name: Balsaminaceae (Balsam Family)

When: June to September

Occurrence: Abundant in the Valley of flowers and indeed all the way along the trek.

Oxyria Digyna, Mountain Sorrel, Chyakulti, Kailashi

Family name: Oxyria (Hillcoat)

Local Name Chyakulti, Kailashi

When: June to August

Occurrence: The long strands of Oxyria Digyna are both in the Valley closer to the Pushpawati river bed, and near Hemkund Sahib.

Note: With a sharp sour taste, the whole plant is used as an appetizer.

Polygonum Amplexicaule, Red Bistorta, Kutrya, Amli

Family name: Polygonum (Linnaeus)

When: July to September

Occurrence: On the way from Gobind Ghat to Ghangaria.

Note: The leaves are used in treatment of wounds.

Polygonum Capitatum, Kaflya

Family name: Polygonum (Linnaeus)

When: June to September

Occurrence: On the way from Gobind Ghat to Ghangaria. This is a ground creeper considered another type of knotweed.

Note: The plant is used as an antidote to Snake poison.

Rhodiola Wallichiana

Family name: Crassulaceae (Stone Corp Family)

When: June to August

Occurrence: On the banks of Hemkund Lake and in the deeper part of Valley of Flowers.

Senecio Graciliflorus, Ground Sel, Kikret, Kuchee

Family name: Senecio (Linnaeus)

When: June to October

Occurrence: About two kilometers from the entry gate of Valley of Flowers. This plant is found an altitude range of 2100–4100 m. This is a rare plant.

Bistorta Vaccinifolia, Inuri

Family name: Bistorta (Scopoli)

When: July to September

Occurrence: Abundant in the further part of the Valley of Flowers. This plant grows near streams and wet places, generally on rocky ledges.

Leycesteria Formosa, Himalayan Honey Suckle, Gulnar, Piralu

Family name: Caprifoliaceae (Honey Suckle Family)

When: June to August

Occurrence: On the way from Gobind Ghat to Ghangaria. And near the village of Ghangaria.

Note: The leaves are ground into a paste used to treatDandruff and kill lice.

Spiranthes Sinensis, Phirlya

Family name: Sipranthes

When: July to September

Occurrence: This is a late bloomer, in the area after crossing the bridge near the entry gate of Valley of Flowers.

Vigna Vexillata, Machali

Family name: Vigna Savi (Snail Vine)

When: Throughout the year

Occurrence: On the way from Gobind Ghat to Ghangaria.

Note: Roots are edible, seeds are used as vegetable and the whole plany is used as a fodder.

Gymnadenia Orchidis, Himalayan Fragrant Orchid

Family name: Orchidaceae.

When: June to August

Occurrence: Deeper in the Valley of Flowers, near the second zone.

APPENDIX I

A short list of the rare green flowers.

All plants in the Valley of Flowers National Park are protected by law. Do not pluck or destroy any part of the plant.

More information and photographs here:

https://susanjagannath.com/vof-bonus/

Angelica Archangelica, Holy Ghost, Wild Celery, Chanda

Family name: Apiaceae (Coriander Family)

When: May to September

Occurrence: This giant flower blooms in the main part of Valley of Flowers in abundance in July.

Note: Archangelica means powerful angel, referring to the powerful medicinal properties of the plant. Angelica has a pleasant perfume closer to the perfume of musk and juniper. Angelica archangelica roots are among the most common botanicals used in gin distillation, often used in concert with juniper berries and coriander as a chief aromatic character-istic for gin.

Saussurea Obvallata, Sacred Lotus, Brahmakamal, Kapfu, Kon

Family: Saussurea

When: July to Mid September

Occurrence: On the way to Hemkund Sahib Lake

Note: The plant is considered as sacred and is endangered.

Codonopsis Rotundifolia, Codonopsis Rotundifolia, Bellwort

Family name: Codonopsis

When: July to August.

Occurrence: Blooms abundantly in Valley of Flowers. Easy to spot in the month of July and August.

Silene Vulgaris, bladder campion or maidenstears

Family: Caryophyllaceae

When: June to September

Occurrence: Throughout in Valley of Flowers after Baman Daur. On both sides of the cobbled path in Valley of Flowers.

Arisaema Propinquum

Arisaema–Propinquum,Cobra lily.

Family name: Arisaema Propinquum (Schott)

When: June to July

Occurrence: On the route from the helipad to Ghangaria, in the forest. And in the forested area after the entry gate.

Feritillaria Roylei, East Himalayan Fritillary, Kakoli, Kshira Kakoli

Family name: Fritillaria Linnaeus

When: June to July

Occurrence: In abundance after crossing the boulder at Baman Daur.

Note: The tubers of the plant are used to treat asthma, fever and tuberculosis.

Polygonatum Verticillatum, Whorled Solomon's Seal, Kantula, Meda

Family name: Polygonatum (Miller)

When: June to September

Occurrence: Within the valley, about three kilometers from the entry gate.

Pleurospermum Candollii, Supka

Family name: Pleurospermum (Hoffemeister)

When: June to September

Occurrence: Hemkund Sahib Lake at an altitude range of 3500–4800 m.

PART VI

More Adventures

CHASING HIMALAYAN DREAMS
A FREE EXTRACT

"I have spread my dreams under your feet;

Tread softly because you tread on my dreams."

— *W. B. Yeats*

SANDAKPHU IS THE HIMALAYAN dream that I've been chasing all my life. This is the story of that dream and how it became a reality. Did you have a dream at 16 that is buried deep under the messy muddle of more important things? I caught glimpses of this impossible, ridiculous and useless dream over the years. A dream the size of Kanchenjunga is hard to ignore forever.

This dream is not about a goal, an achievement, or about doing – it is only about the right place, at the right time, to do nothing at all but be in a waking dream as close to the white heat of a sacred mountain as possible. To gaze on towering Kanchenjunga and the Sleeping Buddha nestled in a snow-white blanket against brilliant blue skies, where the stain of pollution is blown away by wild Himalayan winds.

I must walk five days and 61 kilometers to do this. Three days up and two days down. Touching 4000 meters. That's *meters* not feet. In the wafer-thin air, you are grateful for every breath of air, unseen, clean, and scarce. I'm not sure if this is a dream too late. Time is running out for all the adventures I'd planned to have as a child.

In late childhood, my favorite book alternated between Rudyard Kipling's *Kim*, and Tolkien's *The Hobbit*, both classic quest stories. On long winter afternoons, I'd laze on the stone benches warmed by the sun and plot out, complete with complicated maps, how I could cycle from Lucknow to London, or take a train from Vladivostok to Venice. But, none of those happened. Why? The responsibilities of adulthood. Marriage, childrearing and career, and as the years raced by, I forgot the dreams of my younger self, until my youngest child finished school. And a slot of time opened, for the forgotten things, like dreams of mountains and long winding trails.

I love being an older woman in India, free from the attentions of the rampant roadside Romeos and ever-present lechers, no perverse sexual innuendos, or 'eve-teasing". "Eve teasing" is the euphemism for low grade continuous molestation; that sexual gauntlet that every woman must run in India, every single day. Every woman and girl knows the rules of public behavior. No eye contact, no smiles, elbows out, no reaction - and even that can be insufficient protection. Then, when you cross fifty, a blessed cloak of invisibility descends, and you can venture out without being jostled "by mistake," leered at or subjected to lewd propositions. Which brings me back to why it took me so long to get to Sandakphu.

I first saw Kanchenjunga at 16 in Darjeeling. 16, the perfect age to fall in love. I yearned to escape the confines of the convent hostel and the reeking chaos of the bazaar for the real mountains; but neither the nuns in the hostel nor my parents would give me permission. A girl alone? Impossible! No, not even a group of girls together. Unthinkable. Orgies? Drinking? Sex? No. A trek?

Read the full book.

THE CAMINO INGLES

A FREE EXTRACT

Two roads diverged in a wood, and I—I took the one less traveled by, AND that has made all the difference.

—*Robert Frost*

MORE PEOPLE HAVE HEARD of the Camino Francés than of the less popular Camino Inglés, or English Way, of St. James, despite that, the popularity of the Inglés has soared in the last few years, as more walkers discover this quiet, green route through Galicia in Northwest Spain. The Camino Inglés, an authentic pilgrimage route, dates from medieval times, when English and Northern European pilgrims sailed to the royal seaport of A Coruña or Ferrol, and then walked to Santiago. It is also called the Celtic Way, as it was the preferred route for Irish pilgrims, who disembarked at A Coruna. As the Camino Francés gets more and more commercialised, the Camino Ingles gets more attractive to those seeking a different Camino experience.

This book describes the route from Ferrol to Santiago. In addition, I have included some of the older paths that are more rural. When I walked the Inglés in early 2019, I found that the Inglés now has a lot of bitumen walking. Yes, the roads may be quiet, but who wants to walk on bitumen when you can meander along muddy paths and leaf strewn forest?

The compostela is the certificate (in Latin) awarded to pilgrims who produce their *credencial*, or pilgrim's passport, at the Pilgrim's Office in Santiago, stamped at least twice a day with a sello from the church, albergue, hostal or hotel. Most pilgrims take every opportunity to get several sellos a day, from bars, cafés and churches.

Note for pilgrims starting from A Coruña: If your *credencial* has two *sello*s a day, for 25 km, in your home country, the Pilgrims Office in Santiago will issue you a *compostela*. In recent years, pilgrims have done this from places as diverse as Ireland and Australia.

Read the full book.

THANK YOU!

Thank you for reading *The Valley of Flowers : The Ultimate Guide to a Trekking Adventure in the Upper Himalaya.*

I hope it either makes your Himalayan trek a reality or helps you to live it with me. If you enjoyed this book, please leave a REVIEW on Amazon, or Goodreads.

It will help others to find the book. It also helps me to find new readers. As an independent author, I depend on word of mouth to get my books out there in the world. If you can leave a review on the Amazon store that you purchased the book from, it would fill my heart with joy!

https://bit.ly/SJ-AMZ

Remember to get your bonuses

http://www.susanjagannath.com/vof-bonus

You can also check out my other books on Amazon.

https://www.amazon.com/Susan-Jagannath/e/B01L26RC06/

ABOUT THE AUTHOR

Susan Jagannath successfully combined a passion for reading, a love of writing and a fascination for technology, to create a career in technical writing before her decision to switch to writing the books she wanted to write. With over 50 technical manuals (not) to her name, it was time to do something different, set off on adventures, help others to have adventures, and write books under her own name.

As an army brat, her childhood included seven different schools, three universities and a couple of emergency evacuations from conflict zones. Travel and adventure were normal. She believes in seizing every opportunity to have a new adventure. Whether it's camping on the beach in Australia, trekking in the Himalayas, kayaking in Queensland, whitewater rafting down the Ganges, or walking the Camino in Spain, her philosophy is to pack it into one or two weeks to create memories for a lifetime, preferable with family and friends.

Susan is now on her next adventure; writing books that are not technical manuals, helping others write and publish, and planning her next getaway, always.

If you are interested in finding out more about Susan Jagannath's books, email her at

susan@susanjagannath.com

DEDICATION

To all the friends and family who travelled with me, physically and virtually, especially my husband, Keith, who comes along for the adventures.

This hike would not have happened without three of my dearest friends, Anju, Shanti and Vibha. The ten days we spent together were sheer magic.

A special thanks to my sister Maureen who is a constant source of encouragement and innovative ideas for production.

THE STREET TEAM

A very special thank you to my street team who have supported me from the very beginning, and without whose help I could not have published this book.

NOTES

7. I LIFT MY EYES TO THE MOUNTAIN

1. https://www.ancient.eu/article/831/shiva-nataraja---lord-of-the-dance/

9. BOOTS ON THE GROUND

1. https://economictimes.indiatimes.com/news/defence/replacing-mules-with-new-vehicles-for-army-a-good-idea/articleshow/59088926.cms
2. https://en.wikipedia.org/wiki/Pack_animal Wikipedia

11. FRAGRANCE AND FIRE

1. https://en.wikipedia.org/wiki/Altitude_sickness
2. https://www.livehistoryindia.com/forgotten-treasures/2018/05/24/from-india-with-love
3. The botanical name is "Meconopsis" whereas true poppies belong to the "Papaveraceae" genus.
4. See "The Hobbit" by JRR Tolkien

12. EXCELSIS

1. https://en.wikipedia.org/wiki/Frank_Smythe
2. https://www.theguardian.com/world/2013/nov/23/mallory-body-everest-secret-frank-smythe

13. DEATH IN THE MEADOW

1. https://www.bible.com/bible/1/PSA.121.KJV

15. SAUNTERINGS

1. En.wikipedia.org/wiki/Yudhishthira

16. THE RETURN

1. https://en.wikipedia.org/wiki/Badrinath_Temple